The Spiritist Review
Choice Texts
Special American Edition
Years 1858–1864

The Spiritist Review
Choice Texts
Special American Edition
Years 1858–1864
Allan Kardec

UNITED STATES
SPIRITIST FEDERATION
NEW YORK
2020

The Spiritist Review, Choice Texts – Special American Edition Years 1858–1864
A comprehensive selection of articles about Spiritist phenomena, events and research in the USA

Copyright © 2020 by the United States Spiritist Council

Original Title: La Revue Spirite – Allan Kardec (1858–1864), excerpts
Translator: Luiz A. V. Cheim
English Editors: John C. Madden and Jussara Korngold
French Editor: Jussara Korngold
This selection was compiled and organized by: Jussara Korngold
(United States Spiritist Federation)
Book Layout & Design: H. M. Monteiro
Cover Design: Paula Wienskoski

ISBN: 978-1-948109-20-8 (United States Spiritist Council)
Library of Congress Control Number: 2020945679

United States Spiritist Council, The Spiritist Review – Special American Edition – Years 1858–1864.
Spirituality, Spiritism, Christianity. Kardec, Allan.
First edition.
First print: October 2020

Contact: info@Spiritist.us (http://www.Spiritist.us)
Book portal: https://is.gd/ussf1

Manufactured in the United States

CONTENTS

The Spiritist Review · Year 1861

The Spiritist Review · Year 1862

The Spiritist Review · Year 1863

The Spiritist Review · Year 1864

Reference

PREFACE TO THE SPECIAL EDITION

THIS SPECIAL EDITION contains a comprehensive selection of articles on Spiritist phenomena, events and research that took place in the USA and were published by Allan Kardec in the issues of *The Spiritist Review*.[1] We have divided the current selection into two volumes. The first volume comprises articles published from 1858 to 1864, and the second one contains those published from 1865 to 1869, to be published at a later date.

Such articles should provide the reader with a more precise idea of all phenomena that were occurring in the USA, and how mediums and reputable people were involved in their research.

Additionally, we have also included a few articles that, although not mentioning the USA specifically, may also help the reader get a broader understanding of some key Spiritist tenets.

All in all, they represent a very substantial introduction to a wide range of Spiritist phenomena reported in great detail from different locations all over the North American continent. Their historic importance for the study and understanding of Spiritism and Spiritualism in the country where these phenomena first took place cannot be overstated, having drawn much worldwide attention in the middle of the 19th century, especially from European researchers.

The Spiritist Review was a much reputed monthly journal written and published by Allan Kardec from January 1858 to April 1869. He died on March 31st, 1869, when he had already finished the April 1869 issue, published soon after his death.

There were 136 monthly issues of *The Spiritist Review*, later bundled in volumes of 12 yearly issues each, composing twelve volumes in total. It is the largest collection of Spiritist writings left by Allan Kardec.

1 See extensive reference section at the end of this book. [USSF]

In his book, *The Mediums' Book*, part I, chapter III, "Methodology," he makes the following remark about *The Spiritist Review*: "An assorted collection of phenomena, theoretical explanations and various articles which supplement what is stated in the previous books (specially *The Spirits' Book*), and which represents in a way the application of it."

While complementing the two main books of the Spiritist Doctrine, and showing their most important applications, *The Spiritist Review* is indispensable to all those willing to have an in-depth understanding of Kardec's thought.

It is the most comprehensive piece of work about the Spiritist Movement in the 19th century, containing the formation and modus operandi of Spiritist groups as well as statistics about its adherents around the world.

In addition to a thorough study of Spiritism and explanations about several issues raised by Spiritists, *The Spiritist Review* shows the evolution of Kardec's thought throughout the development of Spiritist Science. In this respect, it remains the most exemplary collection of texts in which Allan Kardec's lucidity, balance and common sense shine through at every turn.

Jussara Korngold
United States Spiritist Federation
New York – NY
September 2020

INTRODUCTION

The speed of propagation of the strange Spiritist manifestations, all over the world, is a demonstration of the interest they attract. Starting as a simple object of curiosity they soon drew the attention of serious investigators who, since the beginning, perceived the inevitable influence they would have on the moral condition of society. The new ideas which stem from them become more popular daily and nothing can stop their progress as everybody, or almost everybody can have access to these phenomena, and no human power will impede their manifestation. If muffled in one point, they appear in one hundred others. Those, therefore, who would find any given inconvenient in such manifestations, would be embarrassed to suffer their consequences by the force of the facts, as the same happens to new technologies which may hurt particular interests in the beginning but gets naturally accommodated with time.

What was not said and perpetrated against magnetism! However, every blow against it, every weapon which hurt it, including ridicule, collided with reality and only served to give magnetism more evidence. Magnetism is a natural force and facing natural forces man is like a pygmy, like these little dogs barking against everything that scares them away.

What happens to somnambulism also happens to the Spiritist manifestations: if they do not take place in day light and publicly, nobody will preclude them from happening in the intimacy, as each family may find a medium in the household, from the children to the elderly, as they can also find a somnambulist. Thus, what if the first to be found is a medium and a somnambulist? Who can preclude that? There is no doubt that the contesters did not think about it. We insist: when a force is part of Nature, it can be temporarily stopped but never eliminated! Its course maybe only deviated. Well, the force revealed in the phenomena of manifestations, whatever its cause may be, is part of Nature, like magnetism, and will not be destroyed, as the electric force will not be either. It is then necessary that those manifestations be observed and studied in all their phases, in order to realize their governing laws. If it is an error and an illusion, time will tell; if it is the truth, that is like the steam: the more it is compressed the higher its expansion capability. Is it a surprising fact that in the Americas, only in the USA, there are seventeen journals dedicated to the subject, not counting a large number of non-periodical publications; France, the European country in which the ideas mostly found support, does not have one?[2] It would be unnecessary to dispute the utility of a special organization to make the public aware of this new science and prevent it against the excesses of credulity, as well as skepticism. This is the blank which we propose to fill out with the publication of this Magazine, aiming at providing a communication media to those interested in these questions and to connect, through a common bond, those who understand the Spiritist Doctrine, from its true moral point of view: practice of good and evangelical charity towards everyone.

If it were only a simple collection of data, the task would be easy. These multiply everywhere with such a speed that it would yield endless subject matter but the facts, on their own, would become tedious by repetition and specially by similarity. What is necessary to the thoughtful person is something that resonates to their intelligence. It was only a few years ago that the first phenomena manifested themselves and we are already far away from the "turning and speaking" tables which

2 Up until now there is only one journal in Europe dedicated to the Spiritist Doctrine – *Le journal de l'âme* – published in Geneva by Dr. Boessinger. In the USA the only journal in French is the *Spiritualiste de la Nouvelle Orléans*, published by Mr. Barthès. [A.K.]

represented their infancy. Today it is a Science which uncovers a whole world of mysteries; which patents the eternal truths only pre sensed by our spirits. It is a sublime doctrine which shows the path of duty to mankind and uncovers the widest field never presented to the observation of the philosopher. Had we stayed inside the narrow limits of an anecdotal magazine and our work would thus be incomplete and sterile, as the interest would have soon passed.

It is possible that the denomination of Science which we gave to Spiritism will be contested. That Science would not have, without a doubt and in any case, the characteristics of an exact Science and it is precisely in this aspect that those who intend to judge and experiment are in error, as if they were dealing with a chemical analysis or a mathematical problem; The fact that it is a philosophical Science is already enough. Every Science must be based on facts but those, by themselves, do not constitute the Science which is born from the coordination and logic inference of the facts: it is the set of laws which govern those facts. Has Spiritism arrived at the state of Science? If that means a completed Science, no doubt it is premature to positively answer that but the observations are already in large numbers today to allow, at least, the deduction of the general principles, where the Science begins.

The thoughtful examination of the facts and its resulting consequences is, thus, a complement, without which our publication would be of mediocre utility and only offer a secondary interest to the thoughtful person and those who want to understand what they see. Nevertheless, as our aim is to get to the truth, we will welcome all observations directed to us and, as much as allowed by the acquired knowledge, we will try to resolve the doubts and clarify the still obscure points. Our Magazine will thus be a tribune in which, nonetheless, the discussion will never distance itself from the standards of the strictest conveniences. In one word, we will discuss but will not dispute. Language inconveniences have never being good arguments to the eyes of wise people: it is the weapon of those who do not have something better to offer and which turn against those who use it.

Although the phenomena with which we occupy ourselves have been more recently produced in a broader way, everything demonstrates that they have been occurring since the remotest ages. Natural phenomena do not follow the same path as the inventions which follow the progress of the human spirit, while those are in the order of all things; their cause is as old as the world and their effects must have been produced at all times. Therefore, what we witness today is not a modern discovery: it is the awakening of the ancient times, but ancient times cleared from the mystic enclosure which generated superstition: ancient times enlightened by civilization and progress, in the field of positive things.

The capital consequence arising from these phenomena is the communication that men can establish with the beings of the incorporeal world and, within certain limits, the knowledge which can be acquired regarding their future state. The communication with the invisible world is a fact, unequivocally found in the biblical books. The Bible however, on one hand, is not sufficiently authoritative to some skeptics; on another hand, to the believers, these are supernatural facts, given by a special favor of Divinity. Had we not found those manifestations in a thousand of other diverse sources, they would not then represent a proof of generality to everyone. The existence of the spirits and their intervention in the corporeal world is attested and demonstrated, not as an exceptional fact but as a general principle, in St Augustine, St Jerome, St Chrysostome, St Gregory of Nazianzus, and in many other Fathers of the Church. That belief forms, moreover, the basis of all religious systems. The wisest philosophers of the ancient times admitted them: Plato, Zoroaster, Confucius, Apuleius, Pythagoras,

Apollonius of Tyana, and many others. We find them in the mysteries and oracles, among Greeks, Egyptians, Hindus, Chaldeans, Romans, Persians, and the Chinese. We see them surviving all vicissitudes of the peoples, to all persecutions, challenging all physical and moral revolutions of humanity.

We find them later among the soothsayers and witches of the Middle Ages; in the Willis and Valkyries of the Scandinavians, the Elves of the Teutonic, the Leschios and Domeschnios Doughi of the Slavs, the Ourisks and Brownies of the Scottish, the Poulpicans and Tersarpoulicts of the Bretons, the Cemis of the Caribbean; in one word: the whole phalanx of nymphs, good and evil geniuses, gnomes, fairies and elves with which all nations have filled the space.

We find the practice of evocation in the peoples of Siberia, Kamchatka, Iceland, among the native Indians of North America and aborigines of Mexico and Peru, Polynesia and even among the stupid savage of New Holland.

The ignorance of a common principle, more or less modified, cannot be due to some absurdities which surrounded or enclosed that belief in various times and places. Well, a doctrine cannot turn universal, does not survive thousands of generations, does not implant from one corner of the planet to the next, among widely diverse peoples, from all degrees of the social scale, if it is not based on something positive. What should that be? This is what the recent manifestations demonstrate to us. Searching for the possible relationships between those manifestations and all those beliefs is to search for the truth.

The history of the Spiritist Doctrine is, somehow, the history of the human spirit. We will have to study it from all sides, providing an inexhaustible source of observations, as much instructive as interesting, about facts that are generally not well known. This will give us the opportunity to explain a number of popular legends and belief, which have their part of truth, allegory and superstition.

Concerning the current manifestations, we will report all patent phenomena that we witness or those which come to our knowledge, whenever we understand they deserve the attention of our readers. We will do the same relatively to the spontaneous effects, sometimes produced among people ignorant of the Spiritist practices, who may reveal an occult power or the independence of the soul. Such are the visions, apparitions, clairvoyance, premonition, intimate warnings, secret voices, etc.

To the report of the facts we shall add the explanations, as highlighted from the set of principles. With that respect we shall reinforce the fact that these principles are derived from the teachings of the spirits, always making abstraction of our own ideas. They do not come, therefore, from a personal theory but from what was communicated to us and of which we are simple interpreters.

Large space will also be reserved to the written or oral communications of the spirits, as long as they have a useful purpose, as with the evocations of past or current personalities, well known or obscures, without neglecting the intimate evocations which, many times, are not less instructive. In a word: we will encompass all phases of the material and intelligent manifestations of the incorporeal world. The Spiritist Doctrine finally offers us the possible and rational solution to a number of moral and anthropological phenomena that we daily witness, whose explanation we would uselessly search for in all other known doctrines. In that category we place, for example, the simultaneity of thoughts, the anomaly of certain characters, sympathies and antipathies, the intuitive knowledge, the aptitudes, the tendencies, the destinies which look like hallmarks of fatality and, in a broader picture, the distinctive character of the peoples, their progress or their degeneration, etc.

To the citation of the facts we will add the research on the possible causes which could have produced them. From the appreciation of the actions, useful teachings will naturally sprout regarding the line of conduct mostly in agreement with the sound moral. In their instructions the superior spirits have always the objective of awakening in men the love for the good, for the practice of the evangelical precepts; hence they shall guide our thoughts which will preside over the writings of this collection.

Thus, the scope of our work comprehends everything related to the knowledge of the metaphysical side of man. We will study them in their present as well as future states, considering that studying the nature of the spirit is to study man, as man will one day participate of the world of the spirits. That is the reason why we will add to the main title the subtitle "journal of psychological studies", allowing for the understanding of its comprehensive scope.

Note: Despite the abundance of our personal observations and the sources from where we collect the facts, we do not dissimulate our difficulties for the task, nor our insufficiency. In order to supplement them we count on the benevolent support of all of those interested in such problems. We shall thus be thankful for the communications transmitted to us about the several subjects of our studies. With that respect we draw the attention to the following ten points about which documents can be provided:

1. Material or intelligent manifestations obtained in meetings where the person was present;

2. Facts about lucid somnambulism or ecstasies;

3. Facts of clairvoyance, predictions, premonitions;

4. Facts relatively to the occult power attributed, with or without reason, to certain persons;

5. Legend and popular beliefs;

6. Facts of visions and apparitions;

7. Particular psychological phenomena which sometimes occur at the moment of death;

8. Moral and psychological problems to be solved;

9. Moral facts, notable acts of devotion and abnegation whose propagation may serve as useful example;

10. Indications of past or modern publications, French or foreign, in which one can find facts relative to the manifestations of occult intelligences, with the designation and, if possible, citation of texts. The same regarding the issued opinions about the existence of the spirits and their relationships with men, from former or contemporary authors, whose names and wisdom give them authority.

Year 1858

SPECIAL AMERICAN EDITION

January 1858
The Mediums' Trial[1]

The critics of the Spiritist Doctrine eagerly pointed to an article published by Scientific America[2] in July 11th of last year under the title "The Tried Mediums". Several French newspapers replicated the article as an irrefutable argument. We have, ourselves, reproduced it, adding some observation which shows its value.

"Some time ago, through the Boston Courier, an offer of $500 dollars was made to any person who, in the presence of and according to the will of a group of Professors from the University of Cambridge, reproduced some of these mysterious phenomena which, the spiritualists say, frequently take place in the presence of agents named mediums."

"The challenge was accepted by Dr. Gardner and several other people who would brag about being in contact with the spirits. The contestants met in the Albion building, in Boston, in the last week of June, ready to test their supernatural powers. Among them were the Fox sisters who were prominent for such events. The examining committee was composed of the Cambridge Professors Pierce, Agassiz, Gould and Horsford, all well-known experts. The spiritualists' trials lasted several days. The mediums had never before seen such a great occasion to evidence their talent and inspiration. However, as the priests of Baal, in the days of Elijah, in vain they evoked their divinities, as demonstrated by the following passage from the committee's report:

"The committee declares that Dr. Gardner, not having been able to present an agent or medium who, from the room next door, would reveal a word requested to the spirits; who could read the English word written inside a book or on a folded

---

1 The original French title is equivalent to "The tried mediums." See below.

2 The actual title that shows in the Scientific American, July 11th 1857 is: *Cambridge Professors and the Spiritualists* - Kardec may have used the expression "tried mediums" because that is how it has likely appeared in the French press of those days. [USSF]

piece of paper; who could answer one question which only superior minds could answer; who could vibrate the piano strings without touching it or even move a small table without the help of hands; as he was unable to give to the committee a testimony of a phenomenon which, even with the most elastic interpretation and greatest good will, could be considered as equivalent to the required proofs; of a phenomenon requiring the intervention of a spirit to be produced, supposing or at least implying such an intervention; of a phenomenon up until now unknown to Science or whose cause was not touchable and immediately recognized by the committee, he has no right to claim from the Courier of Boston the payment of $500 dollars as offered."

This experiment reminds us of another one, which took place in France ten years ago, concerning the pro or con lucid somnambulists, who can generate a magnetic field. The Science Academy had the task of awarding 2,500 francs to the magnetized somnambulist who could read blindfolded. Usually all somnambulists did this on stages or playhouses. They would read from closed books and deciphered letters which were seated upon or well sealed and folded and placed on their chests. In front of the Academy, however, they read absolutely nothing and the award was not given to anyone.

These attempts demonstrate again the absolute ignorance on the part of our critics, with respect to the principles on which the Spiritist manifestations are based. They have the idea that such phenomena must obey the will and repeat itself with a mechanical precision. They forget or do not know that the cause of such phenomena is entirely ethical and that the spirits, who are the immediate agents, do not obey anybody's caprice – medium or otherwise.

The spirits act when they wish to do so and before whom they please. At times, when least expected, their manifestations take place with more energy and, whenever requested, they do not occur.

The spirits behave in ways unknown to us. What is outside matter cannot be controlled by matter. Assessing them from our point of view is to be fooled. If they find it useful to manifest through particular signs, they will do that but never under our command or to satisfy our useless curiosity.

Besides, one must take into account a very well-known cause which pushes spirits away, namely their dislike for certain people who want to submit their discernment to a trial, framing questions about known things. We assume that when something does exist then the spirits have to know it. Just because it is something known to us or that we have means of knowing it would the spirits bother to answer. Such suspicion irritates the spirits and it turns the serious spirits away who, out of their own will, speak to those who trust them, without ulterior motive.

Do we not have a daily example among us? Superior people, who are conscious of their worth, do not like to respond to naïve questions aimed at testing them on elementary things. How would they react if we argued: "But if you do not answer is that you do not know!" They would turn their back to us. This is what the spirits do.

Then you will say: If that is the case, how can you convince us? Considering the interest of the Spiritist Doctrine, shouldn't the spirits want to make their presence known? We will answer that it is too much pride in someone to consider oneself indispensable to the success of the cause. Well, the spirits do not like arrogant people. They convince whomever they wish and to those who believe in their own importance they show their dislike by not listening to them.

In summary, let us see their answers given to two questions about the subject:

Q – Can one ask the spirits to give us material proof of their existence and power?

A – No doubt certain manifestations can be provoked but not everyone is able to do that and, many times, what is demanded is not obtained. They do not bend to the caprices of the human beings.

Q – But when someone requests proof in order to be convinced, would not be convenient to have this proof so as to have one more example?

A – The spirits only do what they want and what is allowed to them. Talking to us and answering your questions, this attests their presence: this should be enough to the serious persons, who seek the truth in the word.

The Scribes and Pharisees told Jesus: "Master, we would like to see you make some prodigy" to which Jesus answered: "A wicked and adulterous generation asks for miraculous signs! But none will be given except the sign of the prophet Jonah." (Matthew 12:39)

We shall even add that it is a great degree of ignorance as to the nature and causes of the manifestations to consider provoking them for any reward. The spirits despise greed as much as pride and selfishness. This only condition can be a reason for them not manifesting themselves. Know this, therefore, that you will obtain one hundred times more from an uninterested medium than from one moved by profit and glamour and that one million would not stop him from doing what he should not do. If there is something strange is the fact of finding mediums capable of submitting themselves to such trials with the purpose of obtaining money.

September 1858
Family Conversations from Beyond the Grave
Mrs. Schwabenhaus – Ecstatic Lethargy

According to the *Courrier des États-Unis*, several newspapers reported the following fact that seemed to provide interesting material for study.

The Courrier des États-Unis says:

"A German family from Baltimore, USA, has just been taken by great emotion due to a case of an apparent death. Mrs. Schwabenhaus who was ill for a long time had exhaled what seemed to have been her last breath overnight, from Monday to Tuesday. The persons who attended her observed every indication of death: the body went cold, the limbs rigid. The undertakers retired to their rooms after having given the corpse the final care and when everything in the mortuary chamber was ready for the funerals. Exhausted, Mr. Schwabenhaus soon followed them. Deep in his agitated sleep he was surprised by his wife's voice around 6 am. In the beginning he thought it was a dream but once he heard his name several times he could not doubt it any longer. He dashed into his wife's room and the person who was left for dead was sitting on the bed, apparently healthy and stronger than ever before.

Mrs. Schwabenhaus asked for water and later she wished to drink tea and wine. Then she asked her husband to take care of the child that was crying in the adjacent room but he was too excited for that, running to call the others from around the house. The sick lady received friends and servants with a smile; all approached her bed hesitantly. She did not seem surprised with all that mortuary apparatus that hurt her eyes. "I know you thought that I was dead", she said; "however, I was only asleep. During that period my soul was transported to celestial regions. An angel came to pick me up and in a few moments we crossed the space. The guiding angel was my little daughter that we lost last year… Oh! Soon I will reunite with her… Now that I have enjoyed the happiness of heavens I no longer wish to stay here. I asked the angel to allow me to come once more to kiss my husband and my children but she will soon come to pick me up."

At eight o'clock, after kindly having said goodbye to her husband, children and several other people who surrounded her, Mrs. Schwabenhaus definitely died, as attested by the doctors without a somber of a doubt.

That fact caused vivid commotion in Baltimore's population.

The spirit of Mrs. Schwabenhaus sustained the following conversation, when evoked in one session of the Parisian Society of Spiritist Studies, on April 27th last:

1. We want to frame a few questions with respect to your death, aiming at our own instruction.

   — How could I not answer you, now that I notice the eternal truths and know about your needs?

2. Do you remember the particular conditions that preceded your death?

   — Yes. That was the happiest moment of my Earthly existence.

3. During your apparent death did you hear what happened around you and saw the burial apparatus?

   — My soul was much concerned with its forthcoming happiness.

   OBSERVATION: It is known that the lethargic generally see and hear what happens around them and keep its memory when awaken. The reported fact offers the particularity of a lethargic sleep accompanied by ecstasy, what explains the deviation in the patient's attention.

4. Were you aware that you were not dead?

   — Yes but that was painful to me.

5. Can you tell us the difference between the natural sleep and the lethargic one?

— The natural sleep is the appeasement of the body; the lethargic is the exaltation of the soul.

6. Have you suffered during the lethargy?

— No.

7. How did your return to life happen?

— God allowed my return to comfort the afflicted hearts around me.

8. We wish a more material explanation.

— What you call perispirit still animated my terrestrial covering.

9. How come you were not surprised when you woke up with all the arrangements that were going on for your funeral?

— I knew I was going to die. I couldn't care less about all that because I had a glance at the happiness of the elected ones.

10. Returning to your alertness, where you happy to return to life?

— Yes, to console.

11. Where have you being during your lethargic sleep?

— I cannot describe my state of happiness. Human language cannot express these things.

12. Did you still feel on Earth or in space?

— In the spaces.

13. When you came back to yourself you said that the daughter you had lost in the previous year came back to take you. Is that true?

— Yes. She is a pure spirit.

OBSERVATION: From the answers of this mother, everything indicates that she is an elevated spirit. No surprise that an even more elevated spirit was united to hers out of sympathy. However, we should not take literally the expression "pure spirit" that the spirits sometimes attribute to each other. It is a fact that it refers to a more elevated order hence those that are completely dematerialized and depurated are no longer subjected to reincarnation: these are angels that enjoy eternal life. Well, those who have not yet achieved a sufficient level do not understand that supreme state. They can then employ the expression "pure spirit" to designate a relative superiority. We have numerous examples of that. Mrs. Schwabenhaus seems to be in that category. The spirits of mockery sometimes also attribute the quality of "pure spirits" to themselves in order to inspire more confidence in those who they wish to trick and that do not have sufficient perspicacity to judge their language, through which they always betray their inferiority.

14. How old was that child when she died?

— Seven years old.

15. How did you recognize her?

— The superior spirits recognize each other more promptly.

16. Did you recognize her under any form?

— I only saw her as spirit.

17. What did she tell you?

— Come and follow me to the Eternal.

18. Did you see other spirits beyond that of your daughter?

— I saw many others but my daughter's voice and the happiness, which I had a glance at, were my only concerns.

19. Once you returned to life you said that you would soon reunite with your daughter. You were then aware of you near death?

— It was a happy expectation.

20. How did you know?

— Who doesn't know that one has to die? The illness told me that.

21. What was the cause of your illness?

— The displeasures.

22. How old were you?

— Forty–eight years old.

23. When you definitely left life, did you immediately have clear and lucid consciousness of your new condition?

— I had it during the lethargy.

24. Did you experience the perturbation that generally follows the return to the spiritual world?

— No. I was amazed but not perturbed.

OBSERVATION: It is well known that the perturbation that follows death is lower and shorter the more depurated the spirit is. The ecstasy that preceded this lady's death was, by the way, the first detachment of her soul from the Earthly bonds.

25. After your death have you seen your daughter again?

— I am frequently with her.

26. Are you bonded to her for the whole eternity?

— No, however, I know that after my previous incarnations I will be in the dwelling inhabited by the pure spirits.

27. Then your trials are not over yet?

— No, but now they will be happy ones. I can only wait and hope. This is almost happiness.

28. Has your daughter inhabited other bodies other than that when she was your daughter?

— Yes, many others.

29. Under which form are you among us here?

— Under my feminine form.

30. Do you see us so distinctly as if you were alive?

— Yes.

31. Since you are here under the form you had on Earth, do you see us through your eyes?

— No. The spirit has no eyes. I only show up under my latest form to satisfy the laws that rule the spirits when evoked and obliged to return to what you call perispirit.

32. Can you read our thoughts?

— Yes, I can. I will read them if your thoughts are good.

33. We thank you for the explanations you kindly gave us. We acknowledge by the wisdom of your answers that you are an elevated spirit and we hope that you may enjoy the happiness that you deserve.

— I feel happy to contribute with your work. Death is happiness when one can cooperate with progress, as I have just done.

September 1858
Propagation of Spiritism

A worth mentioning phenomenon is taking place with respect to the propagation of Spiritism. Just resurrected a few years ago from the old beliefs, it appeared among us not as before, under the shadow of mystery, but in the open light for everyone to see.

It was an object of brief curiosity to some, an enjoyment put aside like a toy. From many people it was received by nothing but indifference; from the largest number, incredulity, despite the opinion of the philosophers whose names are frequently invoked as authorities. That is not a surprise: Has Jesus himself convinced the Jewish people about his miracles? Have the benevolence and sublimity of his doctrine conquered him any mercy before his judges? Wasn't he treated as an imposter? And, if they did not call him charlatan wasn't that because such a word of our modern civilization was unknown by then? However, serious people have seen something beyond frivolity in the phenomena that take place in our days. They studied them, investigated them, with the eyes of a conscious observer and discovered the key to a number of mysteries hitherto incomprehensible. This became a stream of light to them and behold, a Doctrine was born from those facts, a philosophy and, we can even say, a science, initially divergent according to the point of view or personal opinion of the investigator but with a gradual trend towards a unity of principles. Despite the self-serving opposition of some and systematic rejection of others who think that the light can only come from their brains, this doctrine finds many adepts as it enlightens us with respect to the present and future true interests of humanity. It corresponds to their aspiration for a future which becomes somehow tangible; finally because it simultaneously satisfies their reason and hopes and dissipates the doubts that used to degenerate into absolute incredulity.

Well, with Spiritism all materialist and pantheist philosophies fall by themselves; doubts with respect to Divinity, existence of the soul, its individuality and immortality are no longer possible; the future is presented to us like daylight and we learn that such a future, that always leaves an open door to hope, depends on our will and our efforts through the good actions.

While they could not see in Spiritism more than the material phenomena, the only interest was the spectacle that impressed the eyes. However, once it has been elevated to the category of a moral science, it has been taken seriously as it has spoken to the heart and intelligence. In addition, everybody has found in Spiritism the solution to what they were vaguely trying to find in themselves; confidence based on evidence replaces a pungent uncertainty; from such an elevated point of view where it positions us, things of this inferior world seem so small and petty that the vicissitudes of this planet are nothing more than transient incidents that we withstand with patience and resignation; the corporeal life is nothing more than a brief station in the soul's life. Using the expression of our wise and witty comrade Mr. Jobard, it is not more than an ordinary lodging-house where it is not worth to unpack. In the Spiritist Doctrine everything is defined, everything is clear, everything speaks to reason; in one word, everything is explained and those who deeply study it in its essence find such an intimate satisfaction to which they no longer renounce. That is why it has conquered so much sympathy in such a short time, sympathy not recruited in the narrow circle of a given place but around the whole world. Had the facts not been there to demonstrate, we could judge by our Review, which is only a few months old, but whose subscribers, although not counting the thousands yet, are spread all over the world. Besides those of Paris and provinces we have those in England, Scotland, Netherlands, Belgium, Prussia, St. Petersburg, Moscow, Naples, Florence, Milan, Genoa, Turin, Geneve, Madrid, Shanghai, Batavia, Caen, Mexico, Canada, USA, etc.

We don't say this to boast but to mention a characteristic fact. In order that a recently founded and so much specialized journal be sought in so diverse and separated regions it is necessary that its major subject finds followers or they would not subscribe to it, thousands of leagues away, even if done by the best writer. It is then by its subject that it draws interest and not by its obscure editor. Its objective is therefore serious, to the eyes of the reader. Hence it is evidenced that Spiritism has roots all over the world and that, under such a point of view, twenty subscribers in twenty different countries prove more than one hundred, concentrated in one place only, hence one could not suppose this to be the works of a fraternity.

The mode by which Spiritism has propagated so far does not deserve a less accurate attention. If the press had made use of its voice in its favor by preaching it; if, in one word, the whole world had paid attention to that, one could say that it had propagated like everything else that takes place thanks to a factitious reputation and that one wishes to experiment with, even if just out of curiosity. But none of that has happened. Generally, the press had not given Spiritism any voluntary support. Press neglected it or if on rare occasions spoke about it was to ridicule it and to send its adepts to the asylums, a not very attractive thing to those who had the mere inclination of getting initiated.

Only Mr. Home deserved the honor of some more or less serious references, while the most vulgar events are conversely widely covered. As a matter of fact it is easy to see that, by their languages, the adversaries speak about Spiritism like the blind would speak about the colors: without real knowledge of the facts; without a serious and profound examination and only through a first impression, hence their arguments are limited to a pure and simple denial, thus we cannot elevate their facetious expressions to the category of arguments. However witty those jokes may be they do not represent reason.

However, not everybody from the press should be accused of ill faith. Spiritism counts individually on serious experts and we know several among the most prominent people from the media.

Why then do they keep silence? The reason is the fact that, besides the problem of belief, there is that of personality that is very powerful in our days. Their belief is concealed rather than expansive, as with many others. Besides, they are forced to respond for their newspapers. As such, the journalist is afraid of losing subscribers by openly raising a flag whose color could displease some of them.

Will that situation last? No. Spiritism will soon be like magnetism that was once discussed through whispers and that now nobody is afraid of confessing.

No new idea, however right and nice it may be, implants instantaneously in the spirits of the masses, and the one that did not find opposition would be a remarkable phenomenon. Why would Spiritism be an exception to the general rule? Time is needed to mature the ideas, as with the fruits, but human levity leads us to judge them before their maturation or without the effort to analyze their intimate qualities.

This brings to mind the witty fable "The baby monkey, the adult monkey and a nut". As well known, the baby monkey picks a green nut still in the shell; bites it, making faces, amazed that others may like such a bitter thing. The adult monkey, less superficial and with a profound knowledge of its species, picks the nut, breaks it, cleans it, eats the nut and finds it delicious. A great moral teaching results from that, addressed to those who judge new things just from the outside.

Spiritism had thus to march without any strange support and behold in five or six years it spread out with an almost prodigious speed. Where has it acquired such strength if not on itself? Hence there must necessarily be something very powerful in its principle to be propagated like that, without the super exciting means of publicity. The fact is, as we mentioned above, that whoever takes the time to study it finds what was looking for, what reason would have allowed to foresee: a consoling truth and, after all, hope and true satisfaction.

Thus, the acquired convictions are serious and durable and not frivolous opinions, just born out of a breath and destroyed by another one.

Someone recently said: "I find in Spiritism such a kind hope; it gives me such a sweet and great consolation that every contrary thought would make me unhappy and I feel as if my best friend would become hateful had he tried to subtract that belief from me." When an idea has no roots it may briefly shine, like those flowers that we force to blossom; soon, however, for a lack of support, die and remains forgotten. Nevertheless, those who have a sound foundation grow and persist and become so much identified with the habits that we amaze ourselves for having gone without it for so long.

If the European press did not support Spiritism the same did not happen in America. This is correct up to a point. There is in America, as everywhere else for that matter, a general and a special press. The former gave Spiritism much more coverage than in our case, although less than we suppose. In fact there are some hostile institutions among them. The special press accounts for eighteen Spiritist Newspapers only in the USA, from which ten are weekly and several of large format. From that one can see that we are very late with that respect. But there, as around here, the specialized newspapers address a specific public. It is evident that a medical gazette will not have the preference of the architects or the people of law; thus, a Spiritist journal, with rare exceptions, will only be read by those with knowledge of Spiritism. The large number of American newspapers that cover this subject prove one thing: they have enough readers to sustain them. No doubt that they have accomplished a lot but their influence is, generally speaking, purely local. The vast majority is unknown to the European public and our newspapers only very occasionally provide some transcriptions of their matters.

By saying that Spiritism has propagated without the support of the press, we referred to the general press, the one that addresses everybody, the one whose voice is daily heard by millions; the one that penetrates the most obscure corners; that informs the anchorite in the depth of the desert as it does with the inhabitants of the city; finally, the one that plentifully spreads ideas. Which Spiritist newspaper can pride itself of echoing the claims of the world? It speaks to the persons of conviction but does not attract the attention of the indifferent.

We tell the truth by proclaiming that Spiritism has been left to its own powers and, if it has walked in such long strides by itself, how is it going to be when supported by the powerful lever of the broad publicity? While waiting for such a moment, it moves continuously, setting its landmarks; its branches will find stanchions everywhere; it will find voices whose authority will impose silence to the detractors everywhere.

The quality of the adepts of Spiritism deserves special attention. Are they recruited among the illiterate, in the inferior layers of society? No. Those are little or almost not at all concerned with Spiritism: they may have hardly heard about it. The turning tables may have found some practitioners among them. Up until now its proselytes come from the first layers of society: among the enlightened persons, among people of thought and wisdom. Furthermore, and this is a remarkable fact, the doctors who for a long time struggled against magnetism, easily adhere to this Doctrine. We count them in large numbers, both in France and abroad, which also have a large quantity of superior people, in all aspects: scientific and literary celebrities, high dignitaries, public servants, general officers, business people, ecclesiastics, magistrates, etc... all extremely serious to subscribe to a paper like ours as a pastime, considering that we do not pretend to be funny and that we are even less willing to find only fantasies in our publications.

The Parisian Society of Spiritist Studies is not any less evident proof of that truth, by the choice of persons gathered around it. Its sessions are followed with great interest, with a religious attention and, we can even say, with avidity. However, it only handles grave and serious studies, sometimes very abstract, not experiences aiming at the excitement of curiosity. We speak about what happens before our eyes; however the same can be said about other centers that occupy with Spiritism, having the same principles, hence more or less everywhere – as announced by the spirits – the period of curiosity declines.

Those phenomena allow us to penetrate in such an elevated order of things, so sublime that compared to these grave questions, a piece of furniture that moves or that raps is like a kid's toy: it is Science 101.

As a matter of fact, we now know what to give attention to with respect to the rapping spirits and, generally, to those who produce material effects. They have been called, and with justice, the jugglers of the spiritual world. That is why we associate less with them than with those that can enlighten us.

We can identify four phases or distinct periods in the propagation of Spiritism:

1° - Period of curiosity in which the rapping spirits play the main role, calling attention and preparing the way.

2° - Period of observation in which we are entering and that can also be called philosophical. Spiritism is studied in depth and depurates; tends towards a unity of Doctrine and constitute a Science.

These periods will follow:

3° - Period of admission in which Spiritism will occupy an official place among universally accepted beliefs;

4° - Period of influence over the social order. Humanity, then under the influence of these ideas, will conquer a new moral profile. That influence is, since now, individual. Later it will act upon the masses to the happiness of everyone.

Thus, on one side, we see a belief that spreads all over the world on its own, gradually and without the usual resources of the forced propaganda, and on another hand that very belief that sows roots, not in the lower layers of Society but in its more enlightened part. Shouldn't this double aspect be something very characteristic and give food for thought to those who consider Spiritism an empty dream? As opposed to many other ideas that come from below, shapeless and misleading, and that only slowly penetrate the higher echelons, where they then depurate, Spiritism starts from the top and will only reach the masses when disentangled from the false ideas, inseparable from new things.

We have to understand, however, that among many experts there exists only a latent belief. With some there is the dread of ridicule, with others the fear of personal harm by the conflict with certain susceptibilities that impede them to proclaim their opinions, out and loud. This is puerile, no doubt, and we understand that well. One cannot ask certain people something that nature has not given them: the courage to face the "what will they say about it?" but when Spiritism is present in every mouth – and that time is not far off – such courage will reach the shyest.

A remarkable change, since some time now, is already noticeable with that respect. People talk more openly; they take the risk, and this helps to open the eyes of the adversaries themselves, that inquiry if it is prudent, from the interest of their own reputation, to attack a belief that, willing or not, infiltrates everywhere and finds support on the higher social ranks.

Thus, the epithet of "mad", so much inflicted onto the adepts, starts to become ridicule. It is a common place that becomes trivial, as the mad ones will soon be in larger number than the sensible ones and more than one critic has already changed sides.

As a matter of fact, this is the fulfillment of what was announced by the spirits when they said: "The greatest adversaries of Spiritism will become its most ardent followers and promoters."

October 1858
Phenomena of Apparitions

Sometime ago the Constitutionel and the Patrie transcribed the following fact from USA newspapers:

"The little town of Leitchfield, Kentucky, counts on numerous experts of the doctrine of magnetic spiritualism. An incredible fact that has just happened there will certainly give a significant contribution to the growth of that new religion. The Park's family, composed of father, mother and three children, already at the age of reason, was strongly embedded by the spiritualist's beliefs. Yet, Ms. Harris, who was Mrs. Park's sister, did not absolutely believe in the supernatural prodigies that they incessantly cogitated. This was a real cause of grief among all members of the family and more than once it broke the harmony between the two sisters. A few days ago Mrs. Park was suddenly taken ill by something that the doctors declared themselves incapable of handling from the beginning. The patient was a victim of hallucinations, permanently tormented by a terrible fever. Ms. Harris spent all nights awaken by her side. On the fourth day of the disease, Mrs. Park sat down on the bed, asked for water and started talking to her sister. Strange enough the fever had suddenly gone. Her pulse was regular and she spoke with ease. Ms. Harris gladly thought that her sister was out of harm's way. After having talked about her husband and children Mrs. Park got closer to her sister and said: Poor sister, I will leave you. I feel death is coming closer. But at least my departure from this world will serve to convert you. I shall die in an hour and shall be buried tomorrow. Carefully avoid following my body to the cemetery, as my spirit, covered by its mortal remains, will show up to you before the coffin is covered with earth. You shall then believe in spiritualism."

"After having said those words the patient calmly lay down. However, an hour later Ms. Harris painfully verified that her sister's heart had stopped, as she had announced. Vividly moved by the incredible coincidence between what happened and the prophetic words of the deceased, she decided to follow her recommendations and on the following day she stayed home alone, while everybody else had gone to the cemetery. She locked the hatches of the mortuary chamber and sat on an armchair near the bed from where her sister's body had just left."

"Only five minutes had passed – Ms. Harris said later– I saw something like a white cloud coming out from the back of the room. The form gradually cleared up: it was a woman, kind of veiled; she moved slowly towards where I was; I heard her steps on the floor; finally I had my sister before my astounded eyes …"

"Her face, far from showing the pale looks of death that so painfully impressed us, was radiant. Her hands, whose pressure I felt well, holding mine, maintained the warmth of life. I was like transported to a new sphere, through that marvelous apparition. Supposing that I was already in the world of the spirits, I touched my breast, my head, to ensure my own existence. But there was nothing painful in that ecstasy."

"After staying for a few minutes, just like that, in front of me, smiling but in silence, my sister seemed to have made a great effort and told me with a sweet voice:"

"It is now time for me to go. My guiding angel waits. Goodbye! I have accomplished my promise. Believe and wait!"

The Patrie adds: "The newspaper from where we have extracted such wonderful news did not say whether Ms. Harris had converted to the spiritualist doctrine. We admit that, however, since many people would be convinced by much less."

We add, from our own account, that the report has nothing to cause surprise to those who have studied the effects and causes of the Spiritist phenomena. The authentic facts of such a kind are considerably numerous and have their explanation in what we have said on several occasions. We will have the opportunity to describe others, coming from not so far away as this one.

Allan Kardec[3]

November 1858
The Painting Medium from the USA

Not everybody can be convinced by the same type of Spiritist manifestations, thus the need for the development of mediums of many kinds. In the USA there are those who draw pictures of people who have been deceased from a long time that they had never seen before. Sensible persons who witness those paintings promptly convert, since the similarities are immediately identified. The most remarkable of those mediums is perhaps Mr. Rogers who we have already mentioned[4], a Columbus resident, tailor by profession, with no other professional qualification.

Some educated people who have repeatedly said this about the Spiritist manifestations: "Resorting to the spirits is nothing more than a hypothesis; an attentive examination demonstrates that it is not the most rational neither the likeliest", to those, above all, we offer the following summary of a translated article published on July 27th last, by Mr. Lafayette R. Gridley, from Attica, Indiana, to the editors of the Spiritual Age, who have published the integral version in their August 14th edition.

"Last May, Mr. E. Rogers from Cardington, Ohio, a well-known painting medium that makes portraits of people who are no longer in this world, came to spend a few days in my house. During his short visit he was influenced by an invisible artist that used the name Benjamin West. He painted some

3 Paris. Typography of Cosson & Co. – Rue de Four-Saint-Germain, 43
4 Vol. I, page 239 of the "Spiritualist" of New Orleans

beautiful life-sized portraits, as well as some others of somewhat inferior quality. Here are some particularities with respect to a couple of those portraits.

Mr. Rogers painted these portraits in my house in a dark room. There was a time when, during this event, the medium was under no influence. During this break that lasted about another hour and a half, I used this time to examine his work... Then Rogers fell again in a state of trance, finalizing the paintings.

Although there had been no reference as to the individuals who were portrayed in the paintings, one of the pictures was immediately recognized as being my grandfather, Elias Gridley. My wife, my sister, Mrs. Chaney, followed by my father and my mother, all were unanimous in acknowledging the great similarity: it was a facsimile of the old man, with every detail of his vast hair, his shirt, etc.

As for the other portrait, none of us recognized it. I hung it on the wall in my store, visible to everyone, where it remained for a week without any identification. We expected that someone would tell us that it was from an old inhabitant of Greece. I had almost lost hope of identifying the person in the picture when in that afternoon, during a Spiritist session that took place in my house, a spirit manifested giving me the following communication:

"My name is Horace Gridley. I have left my corporal body more than five years ago. I lived in Natchez, Mississippi, for several years, where I was the sheriff. My only daughter still lives there. I am your father's cousin. You can get more information about me from your uncle, Mr. Gridley from Brownsville, Tennessee. The portrait that you have in your store is mine, from the time I lived on Earth, short before I passed on to this other existence, more elevated, better and happier. The picture resembles me, at least as much as I was able to return to the looks of that time, since that is indispensable while we are being portrayed. We do our best to remember that appearance, according to the conditions of the moment. The portrait in question is not finished as I wished it to be. There are some slight imperfections that Mr. West says are due to the condition of the medium. In spite of that send the picture to Natchez, so as it may be examined. I do believe they will identify it."

The facts mentioned in this communication were completely ignored by me and by all inhabitants of the surroundings. Although many years ago I had once heard that my father had a relative on that side of the Mississippi, none of us knew his name, the place where he had lived; not even if he was alive. It was only several days later that I heard from my father, who lived in Delphi, forty miles from here, that it was the place of residence of his cousin, from whom he had hardly heard over the last sixty years.

We not even thought of requesting family pictures. I had just put a note, in front of the medium, with the names of about twenty former residents of Attica, from whom we wished to obtain the portraits.

Thus, any reasonable person would admit that neither the portrait, nor the communication of Horace Gridley, could be the result of our thoughts transmitted to the medium. As a matter of fact, Mr. Rogers has never known any of the persons that he portrayed and probably never heard about them, since he is an English man; he came to the USA ten years ago and has never traveled south beyond Cincinnati, while Horace Gridley, as far as I know, has never traveled north beyond Memphis, Tennessee, over the last thirty five years of his life. I ignore if he had ever visited England for one day, however this could have happened before Rogers' birth, since he is not more than twenty eight to thirty years old. Regarding my grandfather, who died about nineteen years ago, he has never left the USA and he has never had a picture taken.

After receiving the communication above I wrote to Mr. Gridley, from Brownsville. His answer came to confirm what we had heard through the communication of the spirit. I also got the name of the only descendant of Horace Gridley, Mrs. L. M. Patterson, still residing in Natchez, where her father lived for many years. He died, according to my uncle, about six years ago, in Houston, Texas.

I then wrote to Mrs. Patterson, my recently found cousin, and sent her a daguerreotyped copy of the portrait, supposedly of her father. In the letter to my uncle of Brownsville I did not say anything about the main objective of my investigation, not saying anything to Mrs. Patterson either: the reason for sending her the picture or how I had obtained it or who the portrayed person was. I just asked my cousin if she recognized the image. Her response was that she could not say for sure but assured me that it resembled her father at the time of his death. Later I wrote again saying that we also thought it had been taken from her father, not telling her however how it had been obtained. My cousin's response, in short, indicated that everybody had recognized her father in the picture, before I had told her who it actually represented. Nevertheless, she seemed really surprised that I had a picture of her father while she herself did not have any and that her father had never told her that he had a picture taken of him, from wherever. She always thought that there was no picture taken of her father and was really happy with my mail, particularly because of her children who had real veneration for the memory of their grandfather.

I then sent her the original painting, authorizing her to keep it, in case she liked it, but did not tell her how it was obtained. These are the main lines of her answer:

"I received your letter and the picture of my father which you allowed me to keep if I find that it does look like him. Truly, it is a lot like him, I will then keep this one for which I am very grateful to you, since I had never had any other image of him, although I think he was better looking when he was healthy."

Before receiving the two last letters from Mrs. Patterson, and out of pure chance, Mr. Hedges, currently living in Delphi but who was an old resident of Natchez, and Mr. Ewing, recently arriving from Vicksburg, Mississippi, saw the picture and recognized it as being of Horace Gridley, with whom both had been acquainted.

I find these facts very significant to be left unknown; therefore I considered a duty to reveal them, so as to give them publicity. I assure you that when I was writing this article I took the utmost care with its absolute accuracy."

NOTE: We already know the painting mediums. In addition to the remarkable drawings that we gave a sample of, but that represent things whose accuracy is impossible to verify, we have seen mediums, absolutely aliens to that art, executing before our eyes easily recognizable sketches of deceased persons that they had never met. But from there to a finely finished portrait, according to all rules, there is a great distance. Such a faculty is associated to a very curious phenomenon, which we are witnessing right now. We shall report that very soon.

Allan Kardec

December 1858
Apparitions

The phenomena of apparitions are now presented in a kind of new aspect, shedding a powerful light over the mysteries of life beyond the grave. Before moving into the strange facts that we will report, we find it appropriate to recap the explanations given earlier and complete them.

One should keep in mind that during its life the spirit is united to the body by a semi-material substance that forms the first covering called perispirit. The spirit thus has two coverings: one dense, heavy and destructible – the body; the other, ethereal, vaporous, indestructible – the perispirit. Death is nothing but the destruction of the gross covering; it is like the worn clothes that we abandon. The semi material covering persists and constitutes, per say, a new body to the spirit.

Such ethereal matter – interesting to point out – is not the soul, absolutely; it is nothing more than its first covering. The intimate nature of that substance is not yet perfectly known to us but the observation has led us to understand some of its properties. We know that it represents a fundamental role in every Spiritist phenomena; that after death it is the intermediary agent between the spirit and matter, as the body is during its life. This allows for the explanation of a large number of phenomena hitherto inexplicable. We shall see in a following article the role that it plays in the sensations of the spirits. Besides, the discovery of the perispirit, if we can say so, led the Spiritist Science into a huge step in an entirely new route.

But the perispirit, some may argue, isn't that a fantastic creation of imagination? Wouldn't that be one of those suppositions made several times to explain certain effects? No. It is not the work of imagination since the spirits themselves revealed it. It is not a fantastic idea since it can be verified by the senses and can be seen and touched. It does exist; we only gave it a name. We need new words to describe new things. The spirits also adopted it in the communications that we have established with them.

By nature and in its normal state the perispirit is invisible to us but it can go through changes to allow us to see it, both by a kind of condensation as well as by an alteration in its molecular structure. It is then that it can appear to us in a vaporous state. The condensation (we should not take this term formally hence we only employ it for the lack of a better one) can be such that the perispirit acquires the properties of a solid and tangible body. It can, nevertheless, instantly return to its ethereal and invisible state. We can have an idea of that effect by the vapor that can pass from the invisible to a foggy state then to liquid and then to solid and vice-versa. Those different states of the perispirit are the product of the free-will of the spirit and not of an exterior cause. When visible to us it is because the spirit gives to the perispirit the necessary property to make it visible. That property can be extended, restricted and ceased, according to their wishes.

Another property of the perispirit is its penetrability. It cannot be blocked by any matter, passing through them all, like the light passes through the transparent bodies.

The perispirit, separated from the body, takes a determined and limited form which normally is the human body, but that is not constant. The spirit can give it a variety of forms at will, including that of an animal or a flame. As a matter of fact, this capability can be easily understood. Don't we see people that make the most diverse expressions, imitating the voice and the facial looks of other people, to the point of deceiving us; pretending to be fat, disabled, etc.? Who can recognize around town those actors that we only see playing a characteristic role on a stage? If man can thus give to his material and rigid body such contradictory appearances, with even more reason the spirit can do it with a covering, which is eminently flexible and can yield to all caprices.

The spirits generally appear to us showing a human form. In its normal state such a form does not have anything very characteristic, anything that markedly separate one from the others. With the good spirits that shape is, by a rule of thumb, beautiful and regular: long and fluctuating hair over their shoulders, ample mantles surrounding their bodies. But whenever they want to be identified they assume all traces by which they were known, including the outfits, if necessary. That is for example like Aesop who is not disabled as a spirit but if evoked as Aesop, considering that he had several existences prior to that, he will show up ugly and with a hunchback, as well as traditionally dressed. It is perhaps the dressing that is most intriguing; if however we consider that the dressing is also part of the semi material covering, we then understand that the spirit can give to that covering the appearance of this or that outfit as with this or that facial looks.

The spirits can appear in dreams as well as in the waking state. The apparitions in the waking state are neither rare nor new; they have happened at all times and history records them in great number. Without going back to the past, however, they are very frequent nowadays and many people have, at first, taken such visions as hallucinations.

The apparitions are particularly frequent in cases of death from individuals that come to visit relatives and friends. They do not often have a determined objective, but one can generally say that the spirits that appear to us are attracted by mutual sympathy.

We know a young lady that appear many times in her house, in her bedroom, with or without light, men that would come and go, despite the fact that the door would be closed. She would feel so scared that she showed an almost ridiculous cowardice. One day she distinctly saw her brother who was alive in California, giving proof that the spirits of the living beings can cover the distances and show up in a place when the body is in another.

Once that lady was initiated into Spiritism she is no longer afraid since she is aware of the visions and she knows that the spirits that come to visit her cannot do her any harm. It is likely that her brother was asleep when he appeared to hear. If she only knew that she could have established a conversation with him, of which he could have kept a faint impression when awaken. It is also likely that he would then have thought to have dreamt of being close to his sister.

We said that the perispirit can become tangible. We spoke of that when describing the manifestations produced by Mr. Home. It is a known fact that he has made hands appear several times, hands that could be touched as if they were alive, but that would suddenly disappear as shadows, although no complete bodies had yet been seen under such a tangible form. Yet, this is also possible.

In one of our member's family, a spirit has been associated to the daughter of this family. This daughter is a ten to eleven-year-old child who has befriended a handsome young man of the same age. He is visible to her and willingly becomes visible or invisible to the other persons. He does all sorts of errands; he brings toys and chocolates to her; cleans the house; go to the stores for groceries and more expensive items. This is not a legend of the German mystic neither a medieval story. It is an actual fact that happens at this very moment while we write, in a French town, in the core of a very respectable family. We have even carried out interesting studies about this case which provided us with the most original and unexpected revelations. We will address this subject with our readers in a more thorough article to be published soon.

Year 1859

SPECIAL AMERICAN EDITION

May 1859
Bond between Body and Spirit

One of our lady friends, Mrs. Schutz, perfectly attached to this world, who does not seem to be willing to leave it soon, was evoked in her sleep, giving us more than once proof of perspicacity while in that state. One day, or better, one evening, after a long conversation, she said: "I am fatigued. I need some rest. I am going to sleep. My body needs that."

I then responded: "Your body can rest. I do not wish to cause you any harm by talking to you. It is your spirit that is here, not your body. You could then entertain my questions without hurting your body."

She replied: "You are wrong. My spirit separates a little bit from my body, but it is like a captive balloon, tied by ropes. When the balloon suffers the bumps of the turbulent winds, the pole feels the effects transmitted by the ties. My body represents the pole to my spirit, with the difference that it experiences sensations unknown to the pole and such sensations significantly fatigue the brain. That is why my body requires some rest, as does my spirit."

According to the lady's own declaration, she had never thought of that explanation before, which showed perfectly well the existing relationships between the body and the spirit, whilst the latter enjoys partial freedom. We knew well that the absolute separation only happens after death and even some time later. However, that connection had never been so clearly and impressively described to us. Thus, we congratulate that lady who, even in her sleep, has demonstrated to bear such a lively spirit. For us, however, it was not more than an ingenious comparison. The image has lately taken the proportions of reality.

While visiting us Mr. R..., a former resident minister of the USA, together with the King of Naples, a knowledgeable man in matters of Spiritism, asked if we had already observed any distinction between the spirit of a living person and that of a deceased one, as it relates to the phenomena of the apparitions. In short, when a spirit appears spontaneously, be in the vigil state or during the sleep, if we have any means of recognizing if the person is dead or alive. Learning that we had no means other than asking the spirit, he then said that he knew a clairvoyant medium in England endowed by a great faculty, who says that every time a spirit of a living person shows up to him, he notices a shiny trail, starting at the chest of the apparition, traveling through space and not blocked by any material obstacle, terminating at the body. It is a kind of umbilical cord that unites the momentarily separated parts of the living being. He had never seen such a thing when there was no corporeal life. That is how he recognizes when the spirit is of a dead or living person.

The comparison made by Mrs. Schutz came to mind, thus we took it as a confirmation of the fact that we have just reported. However, we will make an observation with that regard.

It is a known fact that the separation, at the time of death, is not sudden. The perispirit detaches gradually while the perturbation stands, keeping some affinity with the body. Couldn't that be the case that the bond observed by the medium, described above, was present at the very moment of death, or a few moments later, as it frequently happens? In that case the presence of the cord would not be an indication that the person is alive.

Mr. R... could not tell us if the medium had made such an observation. In any case it is not less important, shinning a new light onto what we can call the physiology of the spirits.

June 1859
Family Conversations from Beyond the Grave:
Black Father Cesar

Father Cesar was a black free man, deceased on February 8th, 1859, at the age of 138 years, near the town of Covington, in the USA, born in Africa and taken to Louisiana at the age of 15. The remains of that patriarch of the black race were carried to the cemetery by a certain number of Covington's inhabitants and a large number of black people.

Parisian Society, March 25th, 1859

1. (to St. Louis) – Could you kindly tell us if we could evoke Father Cesar that we have just mentioned?

    — Yes. I will help him to respond.

    NOTE: This start leads to a supposition about the condition of the spirit that we wanted to interrogate.

2. (Evocation).

    — What do you want from me? What can a poor spirit like me do in a meeting like yours?

3. Are you happier now than when you were alive?

    — Yes, because my situation on Earth was not good.

4. However you were free. In which sense you feel happier now?

    — Because my spirit is no longer black.

    NOTE: This answer is more sensible than it seems at first sight. The spirit is certainly never black. He means that as a spirit he no longer suffers the humiliations to which the black race is submitted.

5. You lived a long life. Did you take advantage of that for your progress?

   — I felt upset while on Earth but at a certain age I did not suffer enough to be fortunate to progress.

6. How do you employ your time now?

   — I try to enlighten myself and find out in which body I can achieve that.

7. What did you think of the white men when alive?

   — They are good but lighthearted and proud of a "whiteness" that is not their call.

8. Do you eventually consider the whiteness as superiority?

   — Yes, since I was neglected for being black.

9. You said that you are looking for a body with which you could advance. Will you pick a white or black body?

   — A white one since the abandonment would hurt me.

10. Did you really live up to the age attributed to you, of 138 years?

   — I don't know exactly for the reason that you mentioned.

NOTE: We had just made considerations about the age of the black people that could only be calculated approximately since there was no civil registration, especially for those born in Africa.

11. (to St. Louis) – Is it true that the whites sometimes reincarnate in black bodies?

   — Yes. When, for example, a master has mistreated a slave, he may ask to live in the body of a black person, as atonement, so as to suffer the same that he had made suffer, then advancing and obtaining God's forgiveness through that.

November 1859
Should We Publish Everything the Spirits Say?

This question was addressed to us by one of our corresponding members. We answer that as below:

Would that be good to publish everything that men say and think?

Those who may have a notion of Spiritism, however superficial it may be, know that the spiritual world is composed of all those who have left their visible envelope on Earth. By having undressed the carnal person not all of them have, for that reason, dressed the mantle of the angels. Thus, there are spirits of all degrees of knowledge and ignorance, morality and immorality. That is what we cannot lose sight of. Let us not forget that among the spirits, as with human beings, there are frivolous, reckless, joking spirits; pseudo wise, vain and proud of an incomplete knowledge; hypocritical, malevolent and what would seem inexplicable to us, had we not known the physiology of this world, there are sensual, villain and perverse spirits who drag in the mud. Besides, as there is on Earth, there are good creatures, humane, benevolent, enlightened and endowed by supreme virtues. However, since our world is not in first place nor last, although closer to the last than to the first, it then results that the world of the spirits encompasses beings more advanced intellectually and morally than our most enlightened individuals and others in situation inferior to the most inferior people.

Since these beings have a patent mean of communicating with human beings and expressing their thoughts through intelligible signs, their communications must effectively be the reflex of their feelings, qualities and vices. The communications could be, pending on the character and elevation of the spirits, frivolous, trivial, gross, and even obscene or marked by the intellectual elevation, wisdom and sublimity.

They reveal themselves by their own language. That is why one should not blindly accept everything that comes from the occult world, submitting everything to a strict control. A not very constructive collection could be built up from the communications of certain spirits, in the same way that it could be built from the speeches of certain people. We have before our eyes a small English book, published in the USA, which demonstrates that fact. One can say that a lady would not recommend it as a reading to her daughter. For the same reason we do not recommend to our readers.

There are people who find it funny and entertaining. May they enjoy it in their intimacy but keep it to themselves. What is even less conceivable is the fact that they brag about receiving such inappropriate communications. This is always a sign of sympathies that should not be a reason for pride, particularly when these communications are spontaneous and persistent, as happens to certain persons. This does not absolutely allow us to pass hasty judgment on their current morality for we know persons afflicted by that kind of obsession that by no means represent their character. However, as all effects, this one may also have a cause and if we cannot find it in the present, we must look for it in a previous existence. If that cause is not in us, it is outside. However, there is always a reason for us to be in that situation, even if that reason is only a weak character. Once the cause is known, it is up to us to stop it.

Besides these frankly bad communications, which harm any delicate ear, there are others that are simply trivial or ridiculous. Would there be any inconvenience in publishing them? If they are published for their worth there would be a lesser evil. If done so for the study of that kind of communication, with the adequate precautions, necessary comments and restrictions, they can even be instructive, as they may contribute to the knowledge of the spiritual world in all its nuances. With prudence and skill, everything can be said. The harm is in presenting as serious things that shock common sense, reason and conveniences. In such case the danger is greater than thought.

To begin with, those publications have the inconvenience of leading to mistakes persons who are not in a position to examine them, discerning between true and false, particularly in such a new subject as Spiritism. Second, these are weapons provided to the adversaries of Spiritism that don't miss the opportunity of taking advantage of that fact, giving them argument against the high morality of the spirits' teachings, because, let us repeat once again, the harm is in presenting as serious something that is notoriously absurd. Some may even see a profanation in the ridiculous role that we may attribute to certain venerable characters, attributing to them an unworthy language. Those who have profoundly studied the Spiritist Doctrine know well which position to adopt in similar cases. They know that the mocking spirits have no scrupulous in taking over respectable names, but they also know that these spirits only abuse those who enjoy the abuse and who do not know or do not wish to destroy their traps through the means of already known controls. The public who ignores this can only see one thing: an absurd, offered to their imagination as if a serious thing, and because of that, they tell themselves that if all Spiritists are like that, then they all deserve the epithet given to them. There is no doubt that such a judgment is hastily. You justly accuse the authors of levity, telling them: study the subject and do not examine one side of the coin only. There are so many people, however, that judge a priori, not taking the burden of moving one hay straw, particularly when there is no good will, that it is necessary to avoid everything which can give them reason for censorship, having in mind that if malevolence adds up to the lack of good will, which is very common, they will be very happy to find what to criticize.

Later, when Spiritism is vulgarized, more widely known and understood by the masses, such publications will not have more influence than a book of scientific heresies would have today. Up until then, circumspection would never be too much for there are communications which may essentially harm the cause which they intend to promote, in a much greater scale than that of gross attacks and injuries from certain persons. If some were carried out with that objective, they would not be successful. The mistake of certain authors is to write about a subject before having sufficiently studied it in depth, thus giving place to a founded criticism. They complain about the frightening judgment of their antagonists, not aware of the fact that many times they are the ones who give away their weak spot. As a matter of fact, despite all precautions, it would be presumptuous to consider oneself shielded from all kinds of criticism, in principle because it is impossible to please everyone; then, because there are those who laugh at everything, even at the most serious things, some for their condition, others for their character. They laugh a lot at religion. There is no surprise then that they laugh at the spirits, who they ignore. If those jokes were at least witty there would be compensation. Unfortunately, in general they neither shine for their finesse nor for their good taste, nor for their urbanity nor for their logic. Let us then do the best we can, bringing reason and convenience to our side, and then bringing the teasers also.

Everybody will easily understand these considerations, but there is another one no less important, as it refers to the own nature of the Spiritist communications, and because of that we cannot omit it. The spirits go where they find sympathies and where they know that they will be heard. The gross and inconvenient communications, or simply false, absurd and ridiculous, can only derive from inferior spirits. Simple common sense indicates that. These spirits do what people who are complacently heard do. They bond to those who admire their silliness and take them over, to the point of fascination and subjugation. The importance given to their communications, through publicity, attracts, excites and encourages them. The only true means of keeping them away is to demonstrate to them that we do not allow ourselves to be deceived, pitilessly rejecting as suspect and apocryphal everything that is not rational; everything that betrayals the superiority attributed to the manifesting spirit and whose name he uses. Then, when he notices that it is a waste of time, he leaves.

We believe to have responded satisfactorily to the question of our corresponding member about the convenience and opportunity of certain Spiritist communications. Publishing everything that comes from that source without examination or correction, in our opinion is to give proof of a lack of discernment. That is at least our personal opinion that we will submit to the appreciation of those who, uninterestedly by the question, can impartially judge, keeping aside any personal consideration. As everyone else, we have the right of expressing our thoughts about the Science, which is object of our studies, treating it our own way, not pretending to impose our ideas, to whoever it may be, nor treating them as bylaws. Those who share our opinion do so because they believe, as we do, that we are with the truth. The future will tell who is right and who is wrong.

Year 1860

SPECIAL AMERICAN EDITION

May 1860
Varieties
New York's library

The Courier from the United States reports:
"A New York paper publishes a very curious fact already known by a certain number of people and about some very interesting comments that have been made for several days. The spiritualists see in that fact one more example of manifestations from the other world. Sensible people don't go that far to find the explanation, and clearly acknowledge symptoms that characterize hallucination. That is also the opinion of Dr. Cogswell, hero of this adventure.

Dr. Cogswell is the chief librarian of the Astor Library. His dedication to the final stages of construction of a complete catalogue of the library has him using hours of work which should actually been dedicated to his sleep. That is how he has the occasion of visiting rooms alone where so many volumes sit on the shelves. About fifteen days ago, around eleven o'clock at night, he was passing by one side room full of books when he saw, with great surprise, a well-dressed man standing and apparently examining the titles of the books with great attention. In the beginning he thought it was a thief, he then backed up and carefully examined the intruder. His surprise became even livelier when he recognized the visitor as Dr... who had lived near Lafayette-Place, who had died and was buried six months earlier. Dr. Cogswell does not believe much in apparitions and fears them even less. Nonetheless, he thought it to be appropriate to treat the ghost with consideration and raising his voice he said: - Doctor, how come you have perhaps never visited this library when alive and you come to visit it after your death? The ghost kindly looked at the librarian and disappeared without responding, leaving him still perplex in his contemplation.

  — A singular hallucination, Dr. Cogswell said to himself. I might have eaten something spoiled over dinner.

He then returned to work and later went to bed and slept uneventfully. On the next day, at the same time, he felt like visiting the library again. He found the ghost at the same spot as the night before. He addressed him with the same words and got the same outcome.

  — That is curious, he thought. I must come back tomorrow.

However, before returning, Dr. Cogswell examined the shelves that seemed to have the ghost's attention and out of a singular coincidence he identified a large number of both old and new books about necromancy. Hence, the next day and a third time he meets the deceased doctor again, and now varying the question he said:

  — It is the third time I meet you doctor. Tell me if any of these books trouble your resting so that I can have it removed from the collection.

The ghost did not respond as it had not on previous occasions but it disappeared definitely and the persistent librarian returned to the same place, at the same time on several occasions, not finding him ever again. Yet, advised by friends to whom he had told the story, as well as doctors who he had consulted with, he decided to take a break and travel to Charlestown where he spent a few weeks, before resuming the painstaking task that he had imposed upon himself and whose fatigue, no doubt, had caused the hallucination that we have just described."

OBSERVATION: A first observation about the article: the nonchalance with which the detractors of Spiritism attribute to themselves the monopoly of common sense. "The spiritualists, says the author, see in that fact one more example of manifestations from the other world. Sensible people don't go that far to find the explanation, and clearly acknowledge symptoms which characterize hallucination." Thus, according to this author, only people that think like him are sensible people; the others don't have common sense, even if they are doctors, and Spiritism can count them to the thousands. Strange modesty, really, the one that uses the maxim: Nobody is right but only my friends and us.

We still wait for a clear and accurate definition, a physiological explanation of hallucination. However, in the absence of that, there is a meaning that is related to the word. In the mind of those who use that term it means illusion. Well, illusion means lack of reality. According to them it is a purely fantastic image produced by imagination, under some sort of overly excited cerebral. We don't deny the fact that in certain cases it may well be so. What remains to be determined is if every event of that kind occurs under the same conditions. From the examination of the above case it seems that Dr. Cogswell was perfectly calm, as he declares himself, and that no moral or physiological cause had disturbed his mind. On another hand, and even admitting his temporary illusion, it is still necessary to explain how come such an illusion had lasted for so many days in a roll, at the same time of the day and in similar circumstances, since this is not the character of hallucination, per say. Had his brain been impressed by a given material cause on the first day, it is obvious that the cause had ceased after a few moments when the apparition vanished. How could such a material impression be identically reproduced over a period of three consecutive days, with 24-hour intervals? It is regrettable, the fact that the author disregarded this when providing explanations because, no doubt, he must have excellent reasons since he is part of the group of sensible people.

Nevertheless, we agree that in the case above there is no positive proof of reality and that, strictly speaking, we can admit that the same aberration of the senses could have repeated.

However, would the same thing happen when the apparitions are followed by events of some sort of material nature? For example, when well alert people (and not in their dreams) see their absent relatives or friends, who they were not thinking of, coming to announce their passing to them, at the time of their death, can it be said to be a result of imagination?

If the fact of death was not real there would undeniably be an illusion; but when the event confirms the prediction, and that is very frequent, how is it possible that the only thing admitted is silly ghost stories? Besides, if it were an isolated or rare fact one could believe in a game of chance. However, as we have been saying, the examples are uncountable and perfectly confirmed. It is up to the *"hallucinationists"* to bring us an irrefutable explanation and we will then see if their reasons are more demonstrable than ours. In particular we would like to have them demonstrating to us, especially if they consider themselves the owners of common sense and do admit that we have a soul which outlives the body, we would like to have them demonstrating, we were saying, the material impossibility that the soul that must be somewhere, cannot be around us, seeing us, hearing and communicating with us.

May 1860
Varieties
Pneumatography or Direct Writing

Mr. X..., one of our most renowned scholars, was at the house of Ms. Huet last February 11th, with a group of six people who were acquainted with Spiritist manifestations for a long time already. Mr. X... and Ms. Huet sat face to face around a little table chosen by Mr. X... He took a piece of paper from his pocket, completely blank, folded it four times and marked it with an almost imperceptible sign, but sufficient to be identified. He put the piece of paper on the table covered by his white handkerchief. Ms. Huet put her hands over the handkerchief. Mr. X… did the same, asking the spirits to provide a direct manifestation, with an enlightening objective. Mr. X… directed his request to Channing to be evoked for that. Ten minutes had passed when he raised the handkerchief and retrieved the piece of paper in which there was a phrase written on one side, written with difficulty, almost illegible, but showing the outline of these words: *God loves you*. On the other side it read: *God* on the external angle, and *Christ* at the end of the paper. This last word was written in such a way that it showed a hinged mark on the folded paper. A second trial was carried out under the same conditions and after fifteen minutes the paper contained on its lower surface, written in bold characters, the following English words: *God loves you*, and below it read: *Channing*. At the end of the piece of paper it read in French: *Faith in God*. Finally, on the back of the same page there was a cross with a sign similar to a reed, both drawn with a red substance. Once the experiment was over Mr. X… expressed to Ms. Huet his desire to obtain more elaborated explanations from Channing, through her mediumship as a writing medium. The following dialogue was established between him and the spirit:

— Are you here, Channing?

— I am here. Are you satisfied?

— Have you addressed the things you wrote to me in particular or to everybody else?

— I wrote a phrase whose meaning applies to all people. The experiment of writing in English however, is particularly to you. As for the cross, it is the symbol of faith.

— Why have you done it in red?

— In order to ask you to have faith. I could not write it because it would be too long; then I used the symbol.

—   Is the red then the symbolic color of faith?

—   Certainly. It is the representation of baptism by blood.

Observation: Ms. Huet does not speak English and thus the spirit wanted to give another proof that his thoughts were foreign to the manifestation. He did that spontaneously and from his own initiative, but it is more than likely that if one had requested more proof, it would not have been there. It is well known that the spirits do not like to be used as instruments in experiments. The most patent proofs are sometimes given when least expected and when the spirits act freely, they sometimes give more than if they were asked. Whether they have the heart to show their independence, or for the fault of not being able to produce certain phenomena as a contest of circumstances which cannot always be produced by our will. It is never too much to repeat that the spirits have their own free will and want to demonstrate to us that they are not submitted to our caprices. That is why they rarely yield to curiosity.

The phenomena, whatever their nature, are never at our services with any certainty, and no one can guarantee that they will be produced at a given moment and at will. Any person who wishes to observe them must be patient and wait and this is frequently a test of perseverance from the part of the spirits, assessing the observer and the actual intention. The spirits give no importance to the entertainment of curiosity and do not bind themselves but to those who demonstrate their real desire for instruction, doing whatever is necessary to achieve that, without any commercialization of their time and effort.

The simultaneous production of signs in characters of different colors is an extremely curious fact, but it is not more supernatural than all others. We have an account of that in the article Pneumatography or direct writing in The Spiritist Review, August 1859. The supernatural disappears giving place to a simple phenomenon explained by the general laws of nature, and that would be called the physiology of the spirits.

May 1860
Varieties
Spiritism and Spiritualism

The following statement by Cardinal Donnet was given in a recent speech in the Senate: "But today, like in former times, it is true to say with an eloquent publicist, in humankind, that Spiritualism is represented by Christianity."

It would certainly be a strange mistake if we thought that the celebrity speaker in that particular event had understood Spiritualism in the sense of spirits' manifestations. The word was employed there in its true meaning, and the speaker could not have expressed it in a different way, unless he had made use of a paraphrase because there was no other term to express the same thought. If we had not provided the source of our citation, people might certainly think that we had extracted it from an American spiritualist, about Spiritism, equally represented by Christianity, in its most sublime expression. According to that, would it be possible that a future scholar, giving a free interpretation to the words of Cardinal Donnet, would try to demonstrate to our descendants that in 1860 a Cardinal had publicly professed the manifestation of the spirits, before the French Senate?

Don't we see in this fact a new proof that there is the need for a different word for each thing, so that we can understand one another? How many endless philosophical arguments haven't we had due to the multiple meanings of the words! The inconvenience is even worse with the translations, from which the biblical texts show more than one example. If in Hebrew the word day and period were not expressed in the same way, we would not have been mistaken about the meaning of the words in the book of Genesis, regarding the duration of the formation of the earth, and science would not have been cursed for a lack of understanding, when it demonstrated that the formation of the planet could not have been accomplished in a period of six times 24 hours.

August 1860
Spontaneous Essays and Spiritist Dissertations
Knowledge of the Spirits
(Medium Ms. Huet)

There is in the study of Spiritism a serious mistake that propagates every day and that becomes almost the focus of attraction of people towards us; it is the fact that they see us as infallible in the answers. They think that we must know everything, see everything, and foresee everything. What a mistake! Huge mistake! Certainly, since our soul is no longer imprisoned by a material body like a bird in a cage, it soars up into space; the senses of the soul become more subtle, more developed; we see and hear better, but we cannot know everything; we cannot be everywhere since we don't have the gift of ubiquity.

What would then be the difference between God and us if we were allowed to get to know the future and to promptly announce it? That is impossible. We do know more than human beings do, that is correct; we can sometimes read the minds and the heart of those who come to us but our Spiritist Science stops there. Make no mistake then and stop questioning us exclusively to know what happens here and there in your planet, or relatively to a material or commercial discovery or to be informed about what is supposed to happen tomorrow, in politics or business.

We shall always inform you about our condition, about our extracorporeal life, about God's greatness and benevolence, about everything that can be useful to your enlightenment to your present as well as future happiness, but do not ask us about what we cannot and must not tell you.

Channing

November 1860
Spiritist Dissertations
Received or read by several mediums
at the Society

Determination in the Spiritist Work

I will talk about the determination that you need in your Spiritist work. A warning was given to you with that regard. I advise you to study it wholeheartedly and apply it to yourselves because like St. Paul, you shall be persecuted, not in flesh and blood, but in spirit. The incredulous, the Pharisees of our time, will criticize and ridicule you. But have no fear. It shall be a trial to strengthen you if you know to offer that to God. You will see your efforts crowned by success later on. It will be a great triumph to you before the light of eternity, not forgetting that it is already a consolation in this world to those who have lost their relatives and friends. It is a true happiness to know that they are okay and that it is possible to communicate with them. Then, march forward. Accomplish your God given mission and it shall be taken into account the day you appear before the Almighty.

Channing

Channing (William Ellery Channing was born in 1780, in Newport, Rhode-Island, New York)

Year 1861

SPECIAL AMERICAN EDITION

January 1861
Spontaneous Teaching of the Spirits
Dissertations obtained or read at the Society by several mediums

The Voice of the Guardian Angel
(Medium, Ms. Huet)

Every person is a medium; everyone that is prepared to hear has a spirit that guides them to good. It does not matter that some people may communicate with them through some specific type of mediumship and that others may only hear them through their inner voices in their hearts and minds. It does not matter; it is still the familiar spirit that gives them advice. Call it spirit, reason, or intelligence, it is always a voice that responds to your soul and gives you good advice. You don't always understand it though. It is not this reason that drags and crawls as to never moving forward; not this reason that loses itself amidst material interests and bad behavior, but this reason that raises the individual above himself, transporting him to unknown regions; a sacred passion that inspires artists, poets, the divine thoughts that raises the momentum of the philosopher; and leads individuals and groups, a reason that the common crude individual cannot understand, but it approaches a man of divinity more than any other creature; an understanding that he knows how to steer from the known to the unknown, and makes him perform the most sublime acts. Thus, listen to that inner voice, that good spirit who unceasingly speaks to you, then you will progressively begin to hear your guardian angel that reaches out to you from heaven.

Channing (William Ellery Channing was born in 1780, in Newport, Rhode-Island, New York)

February 1861,
Bulletin of the Society, Private Meeting, January 4th, 1861 under the item: Multiple Communications.

2nd – Following the report given by a New York businessman attending the session, Mr. Allan Kardec points out the progress achieved by the Spiritist principles contained in *The Spirits' Book* in the United States of America. Several fragments of the book were translated into English and the doctrine of reincarnation now counts on many followers there.

February 1861
Mr. Squire

Several newspapers, as usual, mocked this new medium who is a fellow country man to Mr. Home, under whose influence multiple phenomena of up to a certain degree of exceptional nature have also been produced. A particular characteristic is that they only occur in absolute darkness, a circumstance duly observed by the skeptical. As we all know Mr. Home produced a variety of phenomena, among which the most remarkable was that of the tangible apparitions. We described them in detail in our February, March and April 1858 issues of this Review. Mr. Squire produced only two, or even better, only one type with certain variations, but not less worthy of our attention. Since darkness is an essential condition to obtain the phenomenon it goes without saying that every precaution is taken in order to ensure the authenticity of the events. Here is what happens:

Mr. Squire positions himself across from a 35-40 kg table, similar to a reinforced kitchen table. His legs are strongly tied up together, to avoid their use. In such a condition his muscular strength is considerably diminished in case he needed it.

Another person, any person and even the most skeptical, holds one of his hands, the other remains free. He then uses that free hand to gently touch the edge of the tabletop. Next the lights are turned off, immediately followed by a movement of the table that lifts it off above his head, landing upside down behind his back onto a couch or a set of previously positioned pillows to protect the table. Once the phenomenon is produced the lights are turned on immediately. It all happens in a few seconds. The experiment may be repeated at will several many times if one wishes in the same session.

A variant of the phenomenon: a person is placed side by side with Mr. Squire; once the table has been lifted and turned as above, instead of falling backwards, it lands horizontally on the other person's head, and that person only feels a slight pressure. As soon as the light is turned back on, the table recovers its full weight and it would then fall unless two other people are prepared nearby to sustain the weight, holding the table from the sides.

That is substantially the report, in its simplest form, without emphasis or reluctance, extracted from La Patrie from December 23rd, 1860 and from a large number of witnesses, here confessing that we have not seen the phenomenon directly. However, the honesty of the people who told us the story gives no room for any doubt regarding its occurrence. We have another perhaps even more powerful reason to admit it. It is the fact that the theory demonstrates its possibility. Now, there is nothing better to reinforce a conviction than the verification. Nothing provokes doubt more than saying: I saw it but I did not understand it. Let us try then to understand it. Let us start by raising some preliminary objections. The first one that easily comes to mind is the fact that Mr. Squire may use some very secretive means or, in other words, he is a skillful con artist; or even that he is a charlatan, as crudely said by those who don't bother to be called rude. One word only is enough to respond to such a hypothesis: Mr. Squire came to Paris as a visitor only and takes no advantage of his strange faculty. Well then, since there is no uninterested charlatan to us that is the most important guarantee of honesty. If Mr. Squire had charged a fee per person, or if he were moved by any interest whatsoever, than the suspicions of foul play would be perfectly legitimate.

We don't have the honor of knowing him in person but we know that he is a very respectable person, with a kind and benevolent character, and we have learned that through other trustworthy individuals. He is a renowned writer, working for several journals in the USA.

The critic rarely takes into account the person's character and the driving force behind their actions. That is a big mistake since such appreciation is of the essence. There are cases in which the accusation of fraud is not only offensive but illogical.

Having said that and leaving aside any presumption of fraud, one needs to know if the phenomenon could be produced with muscular force. Tests were carried out with the support of very strong men and everyone agreed that it was absolutely impossible to lift that table with one hand and even more so to make it spin in the air. We must add that the physical structure of Mr. Squire is not exactly that of Hercules.

Since the use of physical force is impossible, given the circumstances, and that a thorough exam prevents the use of any mechanical means of support, it is then necessary to admit that there is a superhuman action at play. Every effect has a cause; if the cause is not in humanity it is absolutely necessary that it is outside; in other words, in the intervention of invisible beings that surround us, knowingly the spirits.

The phenomenon produced by Mr. Squire is nothing new to Spiritists, with the exception of the way that it is produced; bottom line is that it belongs to the category of all other phenomena of transport and dislocation of objects, with or without contact, of suspension of heavy bodies in the air. Its principle is in the elemental phenomena of the turning tables, whose complete theory can be found in "The Mediums' Book".

Any person that may have given some thought to that theory can easily find the explanation about the effects produced by Mr. Squire. Undoubtedly the fact that a table may lift up, move on the floor, rise and stay in the air without support, without any physical contact, is even more extraordinary. If we can understand these phenomena then we can even more so the phenomenon described above.

One may still ask where the proof of the intervention of the spirits is in all that. If the effects were purely mechanical it is true that there would not be any proof of intervention and in such case the acknowledgment of an electric fluid or similar would be enough. However, since there is proof of an intelligent phenomenon there must be an intelligent cause behind it. Well then, it was through the signs of intelligence of these effects that it was possible to recognize that the phenomena were not purely material. We speak of the Spiritist phenomena as a whole since there are some whose intelligent effect is almost null, as in Mr. Squire's case. He could then be supposed to have a natural electrical potential, like many other people seem to have. However, as far as we know, light has never been an obstacle to the action of electricity or the magnetic fluid. On the other hand, the detailed analysis of the circumstances of the phenomenon rule out such hypothesis, while there is an evident analogy with the other phenomena that can only be produced by the intervention of occult intelligences. It is then more rational to classify it among the latter ones. We still need to know how the spirit is able to act upon matter.

When a table moves it is not the spirit that grabs it and raises it with their hands, for the simple fact that although they do have a body like ours, it is fluidic and cannot exert a muscular action properly speaking. The spirit saturates the table with its own fluid, combined with the animalized fluid of the medium. Thus, the table becomes momentarily animated by a kind of fictitious life. The table then obeys the will of the spirit, like a living creature would do. It expresses happiness, rage and several feelings of the spirit through its movements, serving the spirit. It is not the table that thinks, that becomes happy or angry; and it is not the spirit that incorporates in the table because the spirit does not metamorphose into a table. The table is just a docile, obedient instrument serving the spirit's will, like a baton agitated by a person, and with which the person can make threats or express other feelings. In this case, the muscles sustain the baton but the table, since the muscles of the spirit cannot displace it, is then agitated by their fluids that replace the muscular force. This is the fundamental principle of all similar motions.

One question that seems more difficult at first sight is this: how could a heavy body be moved from the ground and be maintained in the air, contrary to the law of gravity? In order to understand this we need to remember what happens daily before our eyes. It is a well-known fact that there is a distinction between the mass and the weight of a solid body. The mass of a given body is always the same, depending on the sum of all molecules; the weight varies depending on the density of the medium where it is located. That is why a body weighs less in water than in air and even less in mercury. Suppose a heavy table is placed on the floor of a room that is suddenly flooded with water. The table will lift up on its own, or at least a man or even a child would be able to lift it, almost effortlessly. Here is another comparison: let us make a vacuum underneath a pneumatic bell, where there will be no air left inside the chamber to balance the external air; the bell would then become so heavy that even the strongest man cannot move it. However, the mass of the table or the bell has not changed by a single atom, but its relative weight has either increased or diminished due to the density of the surrounding fluid (buoyancy).

Now, do we know every fluid of nature or even all properties of the fluids that are known? It would be presumptuous to admit that. The examples above serve as comparison, but we don't say similarity. We just want to show that the Spiritist phenomena that appear strange to us are not stranger than those mentioned above and can thus be explained, if not by the same causes at least by analogous ones.

In fact, there we have a table that evidently loses its apparent weight at a given moment and that, in different circumstances, becomes overloaded, and such fact cannot be explained by the known laws. Since it is repeated, it then demonstrates that it is submitted to a law that cannot be considered inexistent just because it is unknown. What is that law? The spirits tell us that. However, instead of their explanation we can deduce from analogy, without the need of resourcing to miraculous or supernatural causes. The universal fluid, as the spirits call it, is the vehicle and agent of every Spiritist manifestation. It is said that the spirits may modify its properties, according to the circumstances; that this fluid is the element that constitutes the perispirit or the semi-material wrapping of the spirit; that it can become visible and even tangible. Is it then irrational to admit that a spirit may at some point in time involve a solid body in a fluidic atmosphere whose modified properties produce on that solid body the effect of being in a denser or thinner surroundings? Under this assumption the motion of the heavy table by Mr. Squire is very naturally explained, as every other similar phenomenon.

The need for darkness is more embarrassing. Why would such an effect stop in the presence of the tiniest ray of light? Would the luminous fluid have any mechanical influence here? It is not likely since similar facts do perfectly occur in daylight. Such specificity can only be associated to the special nature of the spirits that manifest through that medium. Why this medium and not others? This is a mystery only penetrated by those who identify themselves with the multiple types of sometimes bizarre phenomena of the invisible world. They are the only ones who can understand the sympathies between the dead and those alive.

What is the category of such spirits? Are they good or bad? We know that we have offended egotistic earthlings by depreciating the value of the spirits who produce physical manifestations; we have been harshly criticized because we classify them as the acrobatics of the invisible world. We apologize and say that this expression is not ours but from the spirits.

We ask for their forgiveness but we could never accept the idea that superior spirits would come to us to have fun, and do stunts and other things like that, in the same way that we cannot be convinced that clowns, circus strongmen, tightrope walkers and jugglers are members of the prestigious Institute (Academy of Sciences of Paris –LC). Those who are aware of the hierarchy of the spirits know that there are spirits of all levels of intelligence and morality, and that is not surprising since the spirits are nothing more than the souls of those who lived here on Earth. Now then, until proven otherwise allow us to doubt that spirits like Pascal, Bossuet and others less elevated may come to serve us and make tables turn, to amuse a group of curious people. We ask those who think otherwise if they believe that they would play such a role after their deaths. Those that operate with Mr. Squire have servility incompatible with the least intellectual superiority, from which we can conclude that they must belong to inferior orders, but this does not mean that they are bad. One can be honest and good and still incapable of reading and writing.

The bad spirits are typically unruly, angry and like to do evil things. Now, we are not aware of any bad behavior carried out by those spirits that manifest through Mr. Squire. They obey peacefully, submissively; a fact that excludes any suspicion of malevolence, but that does not make them capable of giving us philosophical teachings. We are sure that Mr. Squire has enough common sense to preclude himself from being offended by our appreciation. The subordination showed by the spirits that assist him led one of our comrades to say that those spirits knew him from a previous existence, in which Mr. Squire might have had great authority upon them, that being the main reason why they still show a passive obedience now. Besides, one must not confuse the spirits properly given to physical effects, commonly designated by the name "rapping spirits" with those who communicate through knocks. This latter means of communication is an actual language and may be employed by spirits of any order.

We have noted that we met a large number of people who witnessed the experiences of Mr. Squire, but among those who were not initiated in the Spiritist Science many have remained unconvinced, demonstrating that the simple vision of the most extraordinary effects is not good enough to lead them to conviction. They changed their opinion after having heard our explanations. We certainly don't present this theory as the last word and definitive solution. However, since known laws cannot explain the facts, one must agree that the system that we admit is not destitute of likelihood. Let us admit it, if you like, as a hypothesis, and when a better solution is presented we will be the first to accept it.

March 1861
Family Conversations from Beyond the Grave
The Spirit and the Roses
(Sent by Mrs. B... from New Orleans)

Emma D... was a 7-year-old beautiful girl who died after having suffered for six months, hardly eating anything during the last six weeks before her death.

1. (Evocation)
   — A. I am here Ma'am, what is it that you want?

2. I want to know where you are; if you are happy and why has God inflicted such a heavy burden of losing you onto your mother and your sisters.
   — A. I am among good spirits that love me and instruct me; I am happy, very happy. My passage with you was the remains of a physical trial. I suffered but that suffering was nothing; it purified my soul while it destroyed my poor body. I now learn about the life of the soul. I am incarnate but now as a conservative spirit. I live in a world where none of us stays longer than necessary to learn the teachings of the great spirits. Beyond that I travel, preventing disgraces, sending temptations away. I am frequently here. There are so many poor African Americans! I always complained but now I love them. Yes, I do love them, poor souls! Many of them are good, better than their masters, and we must feel sorry even for the lazy ones. Many times I visited my dear mother. Whenever she feels her heart invigorating that is me casting the divine balm on her. She does need to suffer, though! Later it will all be forgotten. And Lucia, my beloved Lucia, shall be with me before long. But the others will come.

It is nothing more than dying to be this way: we change bodies, and that is all. I no longer suffer the illness that upset others. I am happier now and at night I lean over my mom and kiss her. She feels nothing but she dreams of me and sees me like I was before the terrible disease. Do understand Ma'am that I am happy. I wish I could have some roses at the corner of the garden where I used to sleep in the past. You could suggest that to Lucia to have some roses there. I loved roses and I still go there so often! I have roses there but Lucia sleeps every day in my little place and I am also by her side every day. I love her so much!

3. My dear little girl, could I see you?

— A. No. You still cannot see me but look at the beam of sun light on the table. I will cross it. Thank you for having evoked me. Be indulgent towards my sisters. Goodbye. The spirit disappeared, for a moment shadowing the light beam that was still there. As soon as the flowers were placed on her dear spot at the garden the medium wrote the word thanks three days later, with the signature of the child. She then wrote: "Start your letter over again; I don't mind. I am so happy to have a medium. I will come back. Thank you for the roses. Goodbye!"

May 1861
Parisian Society of Spiritist Studies

Allan Kardec's Speech

Beginning of the new social year. Given at the session of
April 5th, 1861

Ladies and gentlemen,
At the time when our Society initiate its fourth year I believe that a special thanks is due to the good spirits who have kindly assisted us and in particular to our spiritual President whose wise advices have helped us to avoid several dangers and whose protection allowed us to overcome the difficulties along the way, which have certainly occurred in order to test our resolve and dedication. Their benevolence – we must acknowledge – has never failed us and thanks to the current elevated spirits of the Society it has triumphed over the ill-faith of its enemies. Allow me a few retrospective observations about this subject.

Experience had showed us regrettable blanks in the bylaws of the Society, blanks that opened the door to some abuse. The Society worked around them and it is to be congratulated ever since. Is it perfect? We would not be Spiritists if we proudly believed so. However, when the foundation is good and all the rest depends on the free-will than all we need is the support of the spirits so that we do not stop half-way through.

Among the most useful changes we place at the top of the list, the institution of free members, giving easier access to candidates, allowing them to be known and assessed before their effective admission as full members of the Society. Participating in all works and studies of the Society, they take advantage of all activities but since they have no administrative responsibility they cannot compromise the Society's liability. Then comes the measure whose objective was to limit the number of attendees to the sessions, with a more strict choice of participants; then the prohibition of reading any message received outside of the Society before its prior analysis, followed by an authorization; finally, those who forewarn the Society against whoever might be a cause of disturbance or who tries to impose their views.

There are others which would be superfluous to mention and whose utility is not less important and whose fortunate results we can appreciate every day. However, if such state of affairs is understood inside the Society the same cannot be said about the outside – and there is no need to dissimulate – where we don't count on friends only. We are criticized on several aspects and although we don't have to worry about it considering that the maintenance of order at the Society is of our interest only, it might not be perhaps totally useless to discuss the points that are criticized because if these are founded we should definitely take them into account. Some people criticize our very restricted admission of observers. They say that if we want to make converts we need to inform the public and for that, we must open the doors to our sessions and authorize any questions and interpellations; that if we don't admit anyone but believers there is no merit in convincing them. This is a tricky argument and if we were to achieve the supposed result by opening the doors then we would be making a mistake by not doing so. Nevertheless, the result would be the opposite and hence we don't do that.

As a matter of fact it would be very unpleasant that the propagation of the doctrine depended on the publicity of our sessions. However large the auditorium might be it would always be very restrict, unnoticeable, when compared to the mass of the population. On another hand we know from experience that true conviction is only acquired through the study, thoughts and continual observation, and not by attending a couple of sessions, regardless of how interesting they may be. Proof of that is the fact that the number of believers who have seen nothing but who have studied and learned is huge. There is no doubt that the desire to see things is very natural and we are far from criticizing it, but we want the conditions to be adequate for people to see. That is why we say: Study first and see later, because you will understand better.

Had the skeptical given more thought to such condition they would have seen, for starters, the best guarantee of our good faith, followed by the strength of the doctrine! The biggest fear of charlatanism is to be unveiled; it fascinates the eyes and is not stupid enough to challenge intelligence that would easily discover the hidden card. Spiritism, on the contrary, does not admit any blind belief; it wants to be clear in all points; wants people to understand everything and be aware of everything. When we recommend study and meditation we are requesting the support of reason, demonstrating that the Spiritist science does not fear examination, for one must understand before believing.

Since our sessions are not designed for demonstrations, its publicity would not achieve the objective and would have grave consequences. With a random crowd, carrying more curiosity than the true desire for instruction, and even further, willing to criticize and make fun of things, it would be impossible to find the necessary silence and reverence required by any serious manifestation.

A somewhat malevolent controversy mostly based on the ignorance of the most elemental principles of the science would establish endless conflicts, when dignity could then be compromised. What we actually want the observers to take away when leaving the Society is that the meeting is dignified, serious, that respects others and expects to be respected, discussing matters with serenity and moderation; that it carries out careful examination, investigating everything with the eyes of a mindful observer who seeks enlightenment, instead of the simple lightheartedness of curiosity. Furthermore, ladies and gentlemen, believe me, such opinion does better to the propaganda than if the observers had left the Society with the thought of having satisfied their curiosity, because the impressions caused by the former lead them to think and the opposite would render them more inclined to laugh than to believe.

I said that our sessions are not for demonstration but if we did that to educate and convince the neophytes, everything would take place in an ambient of seriousness and reverence, as in our ordinary sessions. Controversy would still exist but orderly, instructive rather than tumultuous, and whoever showed a non-civil behavior would be excluded; the focus would not be lost and the discussion would be helpful to everyone. That is what we will probably do one day. People may ask why we don't do that earlier in the interest of propagation of science. For a simple reason: we wanted to proceed with prudence and not like the careless who are more impatient than thoughtful. Before instructing others we wanted to instruct ourselves. We want to base the teachings on an overwhelming mass of facts and observations and not on a few isolated experiments, superficially and lightheartedly observed. Every science forcibly meets facts in the beginning that seem contradictory and only a detailed and thorough study may demonstrate their connection. It was the common law of those facts that we sought in order to show an as broad as possible range, allowing minimal margin for contradiction. It was with that objective that we collected facts, heard and examined them in their inner most details, discussed and commented them with exemption, without enthusiasm. That is how we uncovered the remarkable links between all parts of this vast science that touches the greatest interests of humanity. That was, ladies and gentlemen, the objective of our works, objective that is perfectly characterized by the simple title that we adopted at The Society of Spiritist Studies.

We meet with the objective of instructing ourselves, and not with that of entertainment. Since we don't seek entertainment, we don't want to entertain others and that is why we only want to have serious observers around, instead of having curious ones who might expect to find spectacles here.

Spiritism is a science and as any other science one does not learn it jokingly. Besides, it would be a lack of respect to take the souls that left our world by objects of distraction; speculate about their presence and intervention would be unrighteous and profane.

These thoughts address the criticism of some people when they say that we go back to well-known facts and don't always seek new things. At this point in time it is difficult that the facts don't permeate in the same circle; people forget that facts as important as those that may affect the future of humanity cannot achieve the status of absolute truth but through a large number of observations.

It would be levity to formulate a law only based on a few examples. A serious and prudent person is more circumspect; something must be seen not once but many times. That is why we don't back up before the monotony of repetitions, since the confirmation results from that and sometimes instructive nuances and when contradictory facts are presented, we look for their causes.

We are not in a hurry to give our opinion about the initial data, which is necessarily incomplete. We harvest when the time is right. We may be marching on a slower pace than some people would like however we march with more confidence, and we don't get lost in a maze of systems. We may eventually know less but we know better which is preferable and we can attest what we know based on the testimony of experience.

As a matter of fact, ladies and gentlemen, you must not think that the voice of criticism against the Society comes from friends of Spiritism; that is not the case. That voice is from the adversaries who feel hurt for seeing the Society advancing calmly and with dignity even through the traps that were laid out and still are. They regret the fact that it is difficult to be accepted as a member for they would love to come here to spread disruption. That is another reason why they criticize since their circle of influence is reduced, thus they say that the scope of the matters are insignificant and unimportant because the Society abstains from discussing political and religious issues. They want to see the Society treading on the dogmatic controversy. Well, that is precisely where they betray themselves. The Society has prudently protected itself against malevolence. By hurting its pride they wanted to drag it through a dangerous path but that will never happen. Since it is only involved with questions of scientific interest it has sheltered itself against the attacks and will remain so. Through prudency, moderation and wisdom the Society reconciled the support of the true Spiritists and its influence extends to overseas countries from where people aspire for the honor of membership.

Now, such tribute paid by people that only know the Society by name or by its works or by the achieved respect is a hundred times more valuable than the hastily opinion of the imprudent or the malevolent who want to push it off the cliff and would be happy if they saw it compromised. While I have the honor of heading it all my efforts will be concentrated in that direction. If I had to move away from those guidelines I would then leave it because under no circumstance would I like to have such a responsibility.

In fact, ladies and gentlemen, you are aware of the Society's vicissitudes. Everything that happened before and after had already been announced and everything occurred as foreseen. Its enemies wanted its destruction; the spirits wanted to preserve it since they knew it was useful, and the Society was maintained and will be maintained until the time necessary to accomplish their objectives. If you have analyzed things in detail, as I did, you will not neglect the influence of a superior power that was manifested and you will understand that it all happened for the better good and for its own preservation. There will be a time when it will no longer be indispensable, as it is today. We will then see what needs to be done since the march has already been designed, given all the events.

The most dangerous enemies of the Society are not those from the outside since we can shut the door and the ears on them. The most feared enemies are the invisible ones, who can mingle with us regardless. It is up to us to demonstrate to them, as we have done so far, that they waste their time by trying to impose themselves on us. We know that their tactics is to spread separation, setting the fire of disagreement, inspiring envy, suspicion and creating trivial susceptibilities that generate hate. Let us oppose them with the barrier of charity, mutual benevolence and we will be invulnerable as much against their occult influence as against the diatribes of our incarnate enemies, who are more concerned about us than we are about them and whose names we have the merit of having never mentioned here for reasons of education and for the fact that we have more useful things to worry about. We force nobody to come to us. We welcome with respect and dedication serious persons that in good faith seek enlightenment and those are sufficient for us not to waste our time rushing after the ones who show their backs to us for futile reasons of selfishness and envy. These cannot be considered true Spiritists, despite the appearances; they are perhaps Spiritists that believe in facts but undoubtedly they are not Spiritists who believe in the moral consequences of the facts otherwise they would show more abnegation, indulgence, moderation and less presumption of infallibility. Seeking them would be a disservice since it would reinforce in them the belief in their importance and that we could not move on without them. We should not worry about those who try to stain our images either. People who were a hundred times more worthy than us were also stained and ridiculed. We could not be privileged there; it is up to us to demonstrate by our actions that their diatribes fall in the void and their weapons will turn against themselves.

After having thanked in the beginning the spirits that assist us we must not forget their interpreters for their service, some of them with such dedication and complacence that are never dismissed. We cannot pay them back but with only the testimony of our satisfaction. The world of the spirits waits for them and their every devotion is compensated in proportion to the lack of self-interest, humility and abnegation.

Summarizing, ladies and gentlemen, in the last year our works progressed with perfect regularity, interrupted by nothing. A large number of facts of the highest interest were reported, explained and commented; very important questions were solved; all cases that were exposed to our eyes through the evocations, every investigation that we carried out came to confirm the principles of the science and strengthen our beliefs; several communications of incontestable superiority were obtained through several mediums; from the province and from abroad we received some remarkable communications, not only demonstrating how much Spiritism is spreading but also how seriously it is seen everywhere. There is no doubt that this is a result for which we must feel happy but there is another one not less pleasing which in fact had been predicted since the beginning: it is the unity established in the theory of the Doctrine as we study and better understand it. In every communication that comes to us from outside we find the confirmation of the principles taught by the spirits, and since the majority of people who send them are unknown to us one cannot say that they suffer our influence.

The very principle of reincarnation that had found many contradictors in the beginning because it was not understood is now accepted by the force of evidence and because every thoughtful person acknowledges in that principle the only possible solution to a large number of problems of religious and moral philosophy. Without reincarnation we were held up at every step. It is all chaos and confusion. With reincarnation everything is explained in the most rational way. If that principle still finds some adversaries, more systematic than logical, their number is quite limited. Now, who has invented it? There is no doubt that it was neither you nor I. It was taught to us and we accepted it. That is all that we did. Only a few systems survived out of the many that appeared in the beginning and we can even say that their rare followers are among those who pass judgment after the first impression and frequently according to preventions and preconceived ideas. However, it is now obvious that anyone who takes the burden of doing an in-depth investigation of all questions and assesses cold-bloodedly without prevention and particularly without a systematic denial is inexorably dragged towards the fundamental and prevailing theory by both reason as well as by logic and we can even say in all corners of the world.

The Society, ladies and gentlemen, has not achieved all that alone. Nonetheless, and without vanity, I believe the Society may claim a small part of that. Its moral influence is greater than thought and that is precisely why it has never veered off from the pre-designed line of moderation. It is a fact that the Society is exclusively dedicated to the study, not allowing to be carried away by the self-serving passions that loom around it; that it does so very seriously as any scientific assembly must do; that it pursues its objective unblemished by any intrigue, throwing stones to no one, not even collecting those that are thrown against it. That is undoubtedly the main cause of credit and consideration that the Society enjoys and from which it may feel proud and that gives certain weight to its opinion. Through our efforts, ladies and gentlemen, out of prudence and with the spirit of union that must reign among the true

Spiritists, let us continue to show that the principles embraced by us are not dead letters and that we preach as much by theory as by example. If our Doctrine contains numerous repetitions, the reason is the fact that people find it more rational than the others. I doubt that the same would happen had we professed the doctrine of the exclusive intervention of the devil and the demons in the Spiritist manifestations, doctrine that is totally ridicule today, exciting more curiosity than fear, but on some intrepid people who will soon acknowledge their uselessness.

As it is professed today, the Spiritist Doctrine has amplitude scope that encompasses all questions of morality. It suffices all aspirations and one can say the most demanding reason by anyone willing to study it and who is not dominated by prejudices. It does not suffer from the petty restrictions of certain philosophies; broaden the circle of ideas to infinity and nobody is capable of elevating their own thoughts above that, thus extracting man from the sphere of selfishness where some tried to confine him. Finally, it is supported by the immutable principles of religion of which it is a blatant demonstration. That is undoubtedly what conquers so many educated followers in all countries, and what will make it prevail in a not so distant time, and that despite the adversaries who in their majority are more motivated by interest than conviction. Its fast advancement since it entered the serious philosophical path is a safe guarantor of the future that is reserved and that is announced all over the world, as you know. Hence, let your enemies speak and act. They are powerless against God's will since nothing happens without his permission and as an enlightened clergyman said recently: "If such things happen it is because God allows for the revival of the faith that is fading away in the darkness of materialism."

June 1861

Speech about Future Life
Channing

(Given on Easter Sunday, 1834 after the death of one of his friends)

We have been given a number of times in this Review, spontaneous communications from the spirit Channing that does not contradict his superiority of character and intelligence. Our readers will appreciate below some passages of his texts when alive, using fragments of one of his speeches, whose translation we owe to the kind support of one of our subscribers. Considering that his name is not much known in France we provide a short biography below as an introduction to his discourse.

———

William Ellery Channing was born in 1780 in Newport, Rhode-Island, New York State. His grandfather, William Ellery, signed the famous declaration of independence. Channing was educated at Harvard College, to attend the medical school but his tastes and talents drove him towards a religious career when in 1803 he became the minister of the Unitarian Chapel of Boston. He then remained in that city where he professed the Unitarian Doctrine, a protestant sect that counts on many followers in England and in the USA, at the highest social echelons. He became known for his broad and liberal views and is counted as one of the most prominent individuals in the US given his remarkable eloquence, his many publications and his philosophical depth. A self-declared follower of peace and progress he relentlessly preached against slavery and for that he initiated such a fierce war against that institution, many liberals felt his exceeding enthusiasm was harmful to his own popularity, sometimes seemingly out of place. His name granted him authority among those who fought slavery. He died in Boston at the age 62. He was replaced by Gannet as leader of the Unitarians.

———

"To the great majority of people, heaven is almost always a world of fantasy. It lacks substance. The idea of a world where the creatures have no dense bodies, pure spirits covered by spiritual or ethereal bodies seems fictitious to them. Something that cannot be seen or touched does not seem real to them. That is sad but not surprising for how can people, immersed in matter and its related interests, not cultivating the acquisition of knowledge about the soul and its capabilities, how can they understand a more elevated spiritual life? To the crowds, someone that clearly and happily speaks about future life and about the victory of the spirit against the corporeal decomposition is a visionary dreamer. Such skepticism about heaven and spiritual things is irrational and unphilosophical as shameful."

"And how irrational is the imagination that there aren't other worlds but this one and no other more elevated way of living than ours! Who can doubt, after looking at the boundless Creation, that there exist superior beings or see any irrationality in conceiving that spirits do exist in a less circumscribed way, less bounded than here on Earth, and that there is a spiritual world?"

———

"Those who have left us for another world must cherish an even more profound interest for this one. Their links with the ones left behind improve rather than dissolve. If the future state is a betterment of the present one; if they must grow and expand in intelligence and love, their memories, fundamental power of intelligence, must act upon the past with an ever greater energy, and every lovely affection that we enjoyed here must renew. The idea that this Earthly life would be erased from the memory of the spirit would be the same as destroying its utility; it would be

the rupture of the link between the two worlds and a subversion of responsibility, otherwise how could a forgotten life be reached by punishment or reward? No. We must carry the present with us, whatever the future may be, happy or unfortunate. It is true that the good ones will build new and even stronger and more sacred bonds; however, under the expanding influence of that better world the heart will have a greater capacity to keep the previous bonds while new ones are constructed. He will keep a kind memory of his birthplace while enjoying a more mature and a happier life. If I could imagine that those who have left this world are actually dead for those who stay I would love them and honor them less. A man that forgets those left behind seems deprived of the best feelings of our human nature; and if the just in their new motherland were supposed to forget their parents on Earth; if, approaching God, they were expected to stop putting a good word for them, could we believe that such a change was beneficial to them?"

"One could ask if those in heavens not only keep a cherished memory of the ones left here on Earth but also that are aware of their present and immediate condition. I have no reason to believe that such awareness does not exist. We are used to thinking of heaven as something far away from us, but there is no proof of that. Heaven is the union, the society of spiritual beings. Can't they populate the universe, thus carrying heaven along with them everywhere? Is it likely that those creatures are restricted, like us, by physical boundaries? Milton said:

Millions of spiritual beings walk the Earth both when we wake and when we sleep."

"A new sense, a new vision could show us that the spiritual world surrounds us from all sides. But even if you suppose that heaven is far away, there is no reason to believe that its inhabitants are not close to us and we are visible to them. However, how do we understand presence? Am I not present to those of you that I cannot reach with my arm but who I can clearly see? Isn't that in total agreement with our knowledge about nature to suppose that those in heaven, regardless of their dwellings, may have spiritual senses and organs through which they can see at a distance as easily as we can see what is near us? Our eyes can effortlessly see planets that are millions of miles away, and with the help of Science we can even see the details of their surfaces. We can even imagine a visual organ sensitive enough or an instrument sufficiently powerful to allow for the detection of inhabitants of those far away planets. Why then, those who have already entered into a more elevated stage of their existences, covered by their spiritual bodies, why wouldn't they be able to contemplate our Earth as easily as when it was their own dwelling?"

"That can be true and it is not an abuse to think so. It could be abused. We don't think of the dead as if they were contemplating us with a partial Earthly love. They love us more than ever, but with spiritual and renovated warmth. Their only wish is to see us worthy of reuniting with them in their place of generosity and piety. Their spiritual eyes penetrate our souls. If we were able to hear their voices it would not be a declaration of personal attachment but a lively appeal for better efforts on our side, to a firmer abnegation, to a broader charity, to a humbler patience, to a more loving obedience to God's will. They breathe from the atmosphere of God's benevolence and their mission now is more important than it was here."

"You may then ask: if the dead are aware of the hardships that afflict us, would it follow that there is suffering in that blessed life? My answer is that I cannot see heaven but as a world of sympathies. It seems to me that there isn't anything that may attract their attention better than the misery of their brothers. But if that sympathy may yield sadness on one side, it is far from making them unhappy. In our inferior word, a selfless compassion, together with the power of lessening the suffering of others, is a guarantee of peace, frequently leading to the purest pleasures. Free from our current diseases and enlightened by a broader vision from the divine governance, such sympathy will provide more joy to the *virtues of those blessed beings, and as any other source of perfection, it will increase their happiness. The friends who leave us for that other world are not among strangers; they don't feel the loneliness of someone that has exchanged his homeland for an unknown country. The kindest human words of friendship are not even close to the scores of felicitation that await them at the entrance of that world. There the spirit counts on safer ways of revealing oneself than here. The newcomer feels surrounded by virtues and benevolence and by that intimate feeling of sympathetic spirits around him, and new bonds may be instantaneously created, stronger than those cemented by years of worldly relationships. The most intimate affections in our world are cold when compared to those among the spirits. How do they communicate? Through which language and organs? We don't know that but we do know that as the spirit progresses it becomes easier to them to transmit their thoughts."*

"It would be a mistake to believe that the inhabitants of heaven are limited to the reciprocal communication of their ideas. Those who reach that level enter into a new state of activity, of life and endeavors. We may think of the future state as something so happy that nobody will need help there, that there is no more need for any effort and the good ones have nothing else to do but to enjoy. Truth is, however, that any activity on Earth, even the most intense, is similar to a child's game when compared to the activity and the energy developed in that more elevated life. And that is how it must be since there is no more active principle than intelligence, beneficence, love for the truth, desire of perfection, sympathy for the sufferings and devotion to the divine works that form the widening principles of life beyond the grave. That is when the soul has total awareness of its capabilities; that the infinite truth unfolds before our eyes; when we understand that the universe is a boundless sphere of discoveries to science, to goodness and worship. Those new interests of life, which reduce the current ones to nothing, multiply forever. Hence, one must not imagine heavens

as a motionless community. I envision it as a world of prodigious plans and efforts for its own betterment. I consider that as a society which has to go through successive phases of development, of virtues, power and knowledge, through the energy of its own members."

"The celestial genius is always active, exploring the great laws of creation and the eternal principles of the spirit; unveiling beauty in the order of the universe and discovering the means of advancement for each soul. There are different degrees of intelligence, as with us here, and the most advanced spirits find happiness and progress enlightening the ones behind. The education that was initiated here continues there and a more divine philosophy than the one we learn here revealing its very essence to the spirit, stimulating his joyful efforts towards his own betterment. Heaven has a connection with the other worlds. Its inhabitants are God's messengers in the whole creation. They have great missions to accomplish and given the progress of their endless existence, they may be entrusted with the care of other worlds."

This speech was given in 1834. In those days there was not a word about manifestations of the spirits in North America. Hence, Channing did not know them. He would otherwise have stated that at certain points he only mentioned it as a hypothesis. Nevertheless, isn't that remarkable that this man had foreseen with such accuracy what would only be revealed a few years later, since apart from a few exceptions, his description of future life is in perfect agreement with that revelation? The only missing point is reincarnation and if carefully examined one can see that his speech is close to that, as with the manifestations of the spirits that he remains quiet about since he did not know them. In fact he admits the spiritual world around us, among us, plentiful of solicitudes towards us, helping us to advance. From there to the direct communications there is only a step. He also states that in the celestial world there is no perpetual contemplation but activity and progress; he admits the plurality of the corporeal worlds, but more or less advanced; had he admitted that the spirits could continue their progress in those worlds and we would have the reincarnation right there. Without it the idea of progressive worlds cannot be reconciled with that of the creation of the souls at the moment of birth of the bodies, unless one can admit the creation of more or less perfect souls and then it is necessary to justify God's preference. Isn't it more logical to admit that if the souls of a given world are more advanced than those of another it is because they have already lived on inferior worlds? The same may be said about the inhabitants of Earth, comparing the savage to the most civilized among themselves.

In any case isn't such a description of life after the grave for its logical deductions more accessible to the most vulgar intelligence and acceptable by the sternest reason, and isn't that a hundred times more adequate to lead to conviction and trust in the future than the horrible and inadmissible picture of the endless tortures borrowed from the Paganism of Tartarus? Those who preach such beliefs cannot imagine the number of disbelievers that they generate and the number of recruits sent to the ranks of materialism.

Notice that Milton who was cited in the speech above has an opinion similar to Channing's about the invisible world in our environment that is also the opinion of the modern Spiritists. The fact is, that Milton, as well as Channing and many other notables, were Spiritists out of pure intuition. That is why we tirelessly repeat that Spiritism is not a modern invention. It has occurred at all times because there were souls at all times and the masses have always believed in the soul. Therefore, we can find fragments of this idea in a large number of old as well as modern texts, sacred and profane. Such intuition of the Spiritist ideas is so general that we daily see lots of people who are not at all surprised when they hear about them for the first time. All that was missing was a formula for their belief.

July 1861
A Providential Apparition

The Oxford Chronicle dated June 1ˢᵗ, 1861 states the following:

"In 1828 a ship was traveling from Liverpool to New Brunswick with Mr. Robert Bruce as second in command. As they were approaching the banks of Newfoundland the Captain and his second in command were calculating a full day's route, the first one in his cabin and the second in an adjacent chamber. The two rooms were designed so that they could see and talk to one another. Bruce was very absorbed in his work that he did not notice that the Captain had left his cabin and gone up to the bridge. Without looking he said: "I found a similar longitude, what did you get?" Since there was no answer he repeated the question and again with no answer. He walked to the Captain's cabin and saw a man sitting in his chair, writing on his slate board. The individual then turned and stared at Bruce, who ran to the bridge horrified.

— Captain, he said as soon as he saw him, who is that person in your cabin?

— Nobody, I believe.

— I guarantee you that there is a stranger there.

— A stranger! You are daydreaming Bruce. Who would dare to be in my cabin, at my desk without my orders? You may have seen the boatswain or the steward.

— Sir, there is a man at your desk, writing on your slate board. He stared at me and I saw him more clearly than anyone I have ever seen before.

— He! Who?

— God knows, Sir! I saw a stranger that I had never seen before.

— You are crazy Bruce. A stranger! We have been offshore for about six weeks now.

— I know, but I saw.

— Well then, go and see who that person is.

— Captain, you know I am not a coward. I don't believe in apparitions however I must confess that I cannot bear the idea of going there alone. I would like to have you with me. The Captain then led the way and found nobody. He then said:

— Look now, you had a dream.

— I don't know how it can be but there was someone there and he was writing on your slate board.

— In that case there must be something written then. He took the slate board where it read: "Take the Northeast route."

The Captain then had everybody on the ship, including Bruce; rewrite that phrase, attesting that the writing was unlike anyone else's. They searched every corner of the ship and found no stranger. The Captain had given thought to the mysterious advice and decided to change course and follow the Northeastern route, appointing a man of his personal trust to be on the watch.

Around 3 pm a block of ice was spotted, then a ship with a broken mast and several men on board. As they approached they learned that the ship could not set sail, had no supplies left and everyone on board was starving. Several boats were sent for the rescue operation but as soon as they got on board and to Mr. Bruce's bewilderment, he saw the very man that he had seen in the Captain's cabin in the crowd of shipwrecked men. As soon as the wreckage was attended to and the ship was able to reestablish its course Mr. Bruce told the Captain:

— It seems that I did not see a spirit today, after all. He is alive. The man who wrote on your slate board is one of the passengers that we have just saved. There he is. I swear!

The captain then invited the man to his cabin and asked him to write on the other side of the board containing the mysterious words: "Take the Northeast route". The passenger obeyed although intrigued by the request. Taking the slate board, the Captain showed the written words to the passenger and asked:

— Is this really your writing?

— No doubt and I have just written it here, before your eyes.

— Then the Captain turned the other side of the slate and asked: How about this?

— Yes, it is my writing but I don't know how that could happen since I only wrote on the other side.

— According to my Second officer here, he saw you today, around noon, by this desk and writing these words.

— Impossible – this is the first time I have been on this ship.

They then questioned the Captain of the wrecked ship about what could have happened to that man, and he said: *'All I know is that he is one of my passengers. However, just before noon he fell heavily asleep, waking up an hour later. During his sleep he said he was confident that we would soon be saved, saying that he was aboard a ship and then described in detail, everything that we confirmed moments later. When he woke he said that he had no memory of any dream, just a recall of some sort of unexplained presentiment about a ship that would rescue us. Something strange, he added, is that everything in that ship seems familiar although I had never been there.'*

Mr. Bruce then told the Captain the story of the apparition that he had seen and all agreed that it had been providential."

———

This is a perfectly true story. Mr. Robert Dale Owen, former Minister of the USA in Naples, who also mentions this event in his book, found every possible piece of evidence supporting its truthfulness. Our question is whether this event has any aspect that one can characterize it as hallucination! It is understandable that the passenger had a lot of hope in his sleep, the kind that never abandons people in desperation. The coincidence between the dream and the rescue could still be the result of chance. However, how can one explain the detailed description of the ship? Even if it is still chance, then the writing on the slate board is material evidence. And for that reason, what about the advice to change course and navigate in the Northeastern direction, towards the wreckage? The hallucination supporters should kindly provide us with the reasons for all those events, and using their exclusive system.

In their opinion there is deception in the provoked Spiritist manifestations. But in the event above there is no indication that the passenger was playing a role in a comedy. That is how the spontaneous manifestations, when supported by undisputable testimony, are of great relevance since there is no room for suspicion of any kind. To the Spiritists there is nothing extraordinary about the fact above because they can explain it perfectly well. To the eyes of the ignorant it will seem supernatural, marvelous.

To someone that knows the theory of the perispirit and the liberty of the soul among the incarnated, it is all part of the laws of nature. A critic greatly amused himself poking fun at the story of the man of with his snuffbox published in the March 1859 issue of The Review, saying that it was all the imagination of the sick lady. What is it that is more impossible in that story than in this one? The two facts are explained by the exactly same rule that governs the relationship between spirit and matter. Besides, we ask all Spiritists who have studied the theory of phenomena if, by reading the facts that we have just reported, their attention was not immediately attracted to the mode by which it can be produced; if they did not find an explanation; if, as a consequence of the explanation, their conclusion was not a possibility, and by force of that possibility, if their reason was not more satisfied than if they had to accept it just as a matter of faith, without the support of their intelligence? Those who criticized us for presenting this theory forget that it is the result of long and patient studies, that they could have done the same, as we have, working as much as we did and still do every day; that by providing the means of understanding phenomena we give it a foundation, a reason for its existence, that silenced many critics and contributed by and large to the propagation of Spiritism, considering that people accept it with more good will than something that is understood in opposition to something that cannot be.

July 1861
Mysterious Drawings
A New Kind of Mediumship

Under this title *The Herald of Progress*, from New York, a journal dedicated to spiritualist matters and directed by Andrew Jackson Davies, published the article below:

"Last year on November 22nd Dr. Hallock was invited along with some others to the house of Mrs. French located at number 8, Fourth Avenue, to witness several Spiritist manifestations and to observe the movements of a pencil. Around 8 pm Mrs. French left the living room where the group was gathering to sit on a couch in an adjacent bedroom. She remained there for the duration of the meeting. A few moments after she was seated she fell into some sort of ecstatic state, her eyes were static and delirious. She then asked Dr. Hallock and Prof. Britton to have the room examined. On the bed, across from the place where she was sitting, there was a briefcase tied up by a silk ribbon and also a bottle of wine to be used in the experiment. The paper that was supposed to be used for the drawings was inside the case. We were asked, said Dr. Hallock, not to touch the case or the bottle. Several pencils

and two pieces of elastic gum were also on the bed but there was no drawing paper anywhere in the room.

After the room was searched Mrs. French asked Mr. Cuberton to take the case to the living room where the other guests were located, then open it and remove its contents. There were a number of common sheets of paper and among those, Mrs. French took six of different sizes from Mr. Cuberton's hand, and all sheets were placed on a table in front of Mrs. French. She asked for some pins and took a 5 almost 6 in. paper ribbon and placed it on the lower side of a sheet of paper, then pinning the extremities of the paper to the ribbon. Having done that, someone was then invited to take the sheet of paper and allow the observers to examine it, then asked that person to keep the ribbon and the pins and return the sheet of paper to her. She did the same thing to the other sheets, changing the position and number of pins every time and having the set examined by a different person, aiming at having the paper recognized by the position of the ribbons. Once all sheets were examined and returned to Mrs. French Mr. Cuberton then delivered the wine bottle to her. She laid the sheets on the table and spilled the wine on all of them until they were completely soaking wet, spreading the wine around with her hand. She then dried all of them individually, pressing and turning them, blowing and agitating them in the air. That alone lasted for a few minutes. Once this was completed, she lowered the lights and invited the guests to approach. During the spillage ceremony one sheet of paper was left too dry and she repeated the procedure for that one (the wine was actually a simple mixture of grape juice and sugar, duly authorized by the State and produced in New England). Mrs. French then turned the lights back to normal and invited everyone to sit by her side near the door. Mr. Gurney, Prof. Britton, Dr. Warner and Dr. Hallock were about six feet away from her and the others could see her perfectly well. She then placed one of the sheets on the table in front of her and kept several pencils between her fingers. Dr. Hallock never lost sight of her as he had promised.

It was all set when Mrs. French then warned that the experience was about to begin saying: 'Time'. Then a sudden movement of the hand and for some time, both hands; a distinct noise was heard as if on the paper; the pencils and the paper were thrown away, to a certain distance, on the floor, by a jerky movement. It all lasted 21 seconds. The drawing shows a bouquet of flowers, composed of hyacinths, lilies, tulips, etc.

The same happened to the other sheets of paper. The second one also shows flowers. The third, a beautiful bunch of grapes with its shoots, leaves, etc. It was done in 21 seconds. Number 4 is a branch and leaves containing fruits similar to apricots. The leaves are a sort of moss. Before doing this, Mrs. French asked the observers how long they would allow her to have to finish it. Some said 10 seconds, others less than that. Well, said Mrs. French, on my count of one look at your watches. When she counted 4 the drawing was finished. Attention! One, two, three, four and the drawing was done! The fifth was a shrub of red currants with 12 bunches of unripe fruits, with their flowers and leaves, surrounded by leaves of another species. This drawing was introduced by Mrs. French to Mr. Bruckmaster, from Pittsburg, as if sent by his sister, according to a promise that she had made to him. Two seconds were necessary for that one. Number six, that can be considered the masterpiece of the whole series, is a 9"× 4". It consists of white flowers and leaves painted on a dark background, that is, the drawing was done in the natural color of the paper while the outlines and interiors using colored pencils. With the exception of two drawings produced in the same way but on a different occasion, all drawings are done by pencil on top of a white background. In the center of those flowers at the bottom of the page there is a hand holding an open book, measuring 1" and ¼" × ¾". The corners are not exactly at right angles but what is really remarkable is the fact that the holes made earlier by the pins to facilitate identification of the sheets outline the four corners of the book. On top of the left hand side page it reads: Galatians VI, followed by the first six verses and part of the sixteenth of that Chapter, covering almost the whole two pages with very readable characters in good lighting, with a naked eye or with the use of a magnifying glass. There were more than a hundred legible words. The time spent for that was 13 seconds. When people were able to attest the coincidence between the holes in the paper and the ribbon Mrs. French, still in trance, asked those around to certify what they had just witnessed in writing. People then wrote over the margin of the drawing: 'Executed in 13 seconds in our presence by Mrs. French. Certified, by the signed below on November 22nd, 1860 at number 8, Fourth Avenue and followed by nineteen signatures."

We don't have any reason to doubt the authenticity of the event or to be suspicious about Mrs. French's good-faith, despite the fact that we don't know her. We must acknowledge, however, that the whole procedure may seem little convincing to our incredulous, to whom there would not be a lack of objections, saying that the whole procedure kept some similarity with those of conjuring, that does all that without so much apparent difficulties. We must confess that we agree a little bit with them. The fact that the drawings were made is undisputable. It is only the origin that does not seem to be unequivocally established. In any case, if we admit that not a single trick was used, it is unarguably one of the most remarkable facts of direct writings and drawings, whose possibility is explained by the theory. Without such theory events as these would be promptly thrown into the common ditch of fables or magic tricks. However, for the very reason that it explains the conditions under which such events may take place they help us to become better observers and to not admit them unless we have enough proof.

The American mediums definitely have a specialty for the production of extraordinary phenomena since the press in that country has plenty of facts of that kind, far from what happens with the European mediums. Thus, from the other side of the Atlantic they say that we are still well behind in matters of Spiritism. When we asked the spirits about such a difference they said: *"Each one with their mission. Yours is not the same and God did not give you the least part in the works of regeneration."*

Considering the merit of the mediums by the speed of execution, the energy and the power of the effects, ours are weaker when compared to those; however we know many people who would not exchange the simple and consoling communications that they receive by the prodigies of the American mediums. Those communications are sufficient to give them faith and they prefer the ones that touch their souls to the others that impress the eyes; the moral teachings that give consolation and make them better to the phenomena that cause admiration. There was a short time in Europe when the physical events drew great attention but that were soon replaced by the philosophy that opens up a broader avenue to our minds, tending towards the final and providential target of Spiritism: social regeneration. Each people has its own genius and special tendencies, and everyone within the limits assigned to it, concurs with the designs of Providence., The most advanced shall be the ones that walk faster on the path of moral progress because that is the one who will be closer to God's designs.

July 1861
Exploitation of Spiritism

North America claims, and rightly so, the honor of having been the first to reveal the manifestations from beyond the grave in our times; why must she also be the first to give examples of commerce and among these people, so advanced in so many ways and so worthy of our sympathy, why has the commercial instinct not stopped at the doorway of eternal life? Reading their newspapers we find ads like the ones below on every page:

"Mrs. S. E. Royers, somnambulist, medium-doctor, psychological cure through sorcery. Common treatment if required. Description of physiognomy, morality and the soul of people. From 10am to 12pm, Mon-Thu; from 7-10pm, except Fridays, Saturdays and Sundays, unless previously arranged. Price: $1/hour."

We believe that the sympathy of that medium by her patients seems to be in direct proportion to the amount of dollars paid. It seems unnecessary to provide the addresses.

"Mrs. E. C. Morris, writing medium; from 10am-12pm, and 7-9pm, Mon-Fri."

"J.B. Conklin, medium. Welcomes guests to his salon every day and every evening. Attend at his home."

"A. C. Styles, lucid medium, guarantees accurate diagnostic of disease of a present person or money back. Strictly imposed rules: a lucid in person exam and prescription, $2; psychometric descriptions of characters, $3. Do not forget that appointments are paid in advance."

"To the amateurs of Spiritualism. Mrs. Beck, trance medium, speaking, spelling, knocking and rapping. True observers may schedule an appointment from 9-10pm at her residence. Mrs. Beck is associated as being a very powerful rapping medium."

Would you think that there is such commerce only among obscure and ignorant speculators? Here is the contrary proof:

"Dr. G. A. Redman, experienced medium, is back to New York. He can be found at his home address where he receives as before."

The exploitation of Spiritualism extended even to common objects. We read an ad in the Spiritual Telegraph from New York: *"Spiritual matches, new invention without friction and smell."*

Even more remarkable for that country is the following ad that we found in the Weekly American, from Baltimore, dated February 5th, 1859:

"Statistics of Spiritualism. The Spiritual Register from 1859 estimates as 1,284,000 the number of spiritualists in the USA.

The Register accounts for 1,000 spiritualist speakers; 40,000 public and private mediums; 500 books and brochures; 6 weekly, 4 monthly and 3 bi-weekly journals dedicated to that cause."

The exploiting mediums arrived in England. There are many in London who charge nothing less than 1.25 francs per session. We hope that if they try to come to France the common sense of the true Spiritist will do them justice.

The production of physical effects excites more curiosity than it touches the heart. Hence the mediums with those skills have the tendency of exploiting such curiosity. Those who only receive moral communications of a higher order have an instinctive distaste for anything that may have smell of speculation of any kind. The reasons for the former are two-fold: first, exploitation of curiosity is more profitable because there are a large number of curious people in every country; second, the physical phenomena act less on the moral side thus their scruples are diminished. To their eyes, their skills are a gift that must help them to get by like a beautiful voice is to a singer. The moral question is secondary or inexistent. Thus, once walking that path their self-serving interest develops the skills of astuteness. As a matter of fact, who knows if the customer today will come back again tomorrow? Then, he must be satisfied at any price. If the spirit does not satisfy the customer, the medium will do something that is easier from a material point of view than from a moral or intelligent communication, of elevated moral and philosophical reach. The former ones find recourses in conjuring that is greatly absent in the latter ones. That is why we say that the morality of a medium must be taken into account before anything else; that the best defense against trickery is in the medium's character, his honorableness, his absolute altruism. Whenever there is a shadow of interest, however minor it may be, there is reason for suspicion. Fraud is always disgraceful but when related to moral issues it is blasphemy.

Someone that knows Spiritism only by name and tries to imitate its effects is not more reprehensible than the juggler who tries to imitate the experiments of a wise Physicist. There is no doubt that it would be better that such a thing would never happen but in reality he is not deceiving anyone since his condition cannot be hidden. He only hides the means. The same cannot be said about someone that knows the holiness of what he is trying to imitate with the despicable objective of mystification. This is more than a fraud. It is hypocrisy since one tries to impersonate what one cannot do. One is even more culpable if truly endowed by some mediumistic faculty and uses that to continuously abuse the trust put in him. God knows what is reserved to them, even here on Earth. If the false mediums harm themselves only this would then be a half-evil. The worst part is the ammunition that they supply to the non-believers and the disgraceful behavior shown to undecided persons when such fraud is unveiled. We do not contest their faculties, even some powerful ones of certain mercenaries, but we say that greed is a direct path to the temptation of fraud that must inspire distrust, all the more legitimate, that one cannot see in this exploitation, the effect of zeal for the sole good of the cause.

Even when there is no fraud, criticism may still reproach someone that speculates with something as sacred as the soul of the dead.

Aug 1861
American Manifestations

The *Banner of Light*, a New York journal from May 18th, 1861 brings the following:[5]

"Deeming the following extraordinary facts worthy of being placed upon record in an authenticated form, we forward them

5 Excerpted from the original publication Banner of Light, from New York, dated May 18th, 1861 kindly provided by Ms. J. Korngold of the USSC. [ussf]

to the Banner for publication, with our signatures attached, as evidence that they occurred in our presence, and under the herein stated.

On Wednesday evening, May 1ˢᵗ, we met the medium H.M. Fay, by appointment, at the residence of Mr. W. B. Hallock, in New York. The medium seated himself near a table, upon which were placed a tin horn, a violin and three separate pieces of small-sized bed-cord. The company were seated in a semi-circle in front of the medium, and the table six or eight inches from them, and with their hands joined, which gave every member of the circle the assurance that his neighbors on his right and left, retained their position in every one of the experiments herein related. The lights were then put out and the company ordered to sing. In a few minutes, a light was called for. The medium was found still seating in his chair, with his hands crossed behind him at the wrists, which were firmly tied together, the knots being between the wrists, and the rope being wrapped around each wrist so tightly as to press into the flesh and obstruct the venous circulation, so that the hands became much swollen. The ends of the rope were then passed upon the inside of the back of the chair, and then brought round and tied, one to each of the front legs of the chair. Another rope was found wrapped firmly around his legs, just above his knees, and tied tightly, while a third rope secured his ankles in the same manner. In this condition, we were satisfied that the medium could neither have tied himself, nor could he untie himself, nor use his hands, nor walk, nor rise from his chair. A member of the circle then placed a sheet of white paper upon the floor, under the medium's feet, with a pencil upon the paper. The light was put out, and, almost immediately, the horn was seized by a power of same kind, and struck upon the table and the floor repeatedly, rapidly, and very violently, so as to make deep indentations in the table. A mouth also seemed to be applied to the horn, and conversed through it, freely and rather jocularly, at times, with the members of the circle. The articulation of the words was as distinct as that of a person in the form when speaking through a horn. The sound was that of a full male voice, and the tone somewhat louder than the tone of common conversation. Another voice, fainter, somewhat guttural, and with a less distinct articulation, also, at times, conversed with the company. A light was called for, and the medium was found still in his chair, bound hand and foot, as already described, and his feet within the pencil lines that had been traced around them. The light was again put out, and soon the horn commenced its pounding and its talking as before. The circle was next told to sing, and the manifestations apparently ceased; but at the call for the light, the ropes were found removed from the medium's ankles and knees; his hands, however, were still tied, as already described, and his feet within the pencil lines upon the with paper. Again the light was put out, and again the pounding and the talking through the horn were resumed. Then, followed an order for singing, which was continued for a few moments, when the light was called for, and the medium was found untied, sitting in his chair, with his feet within the pencil lines. This closed the first series of manifestations.

> *The light was again put out, and after a few moments singing by the circle, the light was struck, and the medium was found tied with one rope around his ankles, with another just below his knees, while with a third his wrists were tied in front of him, even more tightly than before, and then lashed to his right tight. A member of the circle then tied his limbs to the chair, and putting a sheet of white paper under his feet, traced with a pencil the outlines of his feet as before. A bell was also put upon the table and the light extinguished, as before, there was pounding upon the floor and table with the horn, and talking through the horn; then the bell was lifted from the table and rung very loudly, about midway between the medium and the circle, and seeming to sweep over an arc of five or six feet at each stroke of the clapper. During*

the ring of the bell the medium repeatedly in a loud voice, exclaimed: "I am here, I am here," thus assuring us that he was still in his chair, while the bell was at a considerable distance from him. The light was ordered, and the medium was found still tied as described, with his feet within the pencil lines.

A large bright spot, an inch and a half in diameter, was now made upon the back of the violin by rubbing it with phosphorus. The light was put out, and very soon the violin rose six or seven feet above the floor and floated rapidly around in the air, making a large sweep at times, of seven or eight feet. In its movements it could easily be followed by the eye, as the phosphorescent spot made upon it was distinctly visible; it was also easily followed by the ear, as its strings were thumbed upon during its flight. As the violin floated around, the medium repeatedly exclaimed in a loud voice: "I am here, I am here," giving us the assurance that he was still in his chair and not following the violin in its movements. The light was called for, and the medium was found tied, as already described, and his feet within the pencil lines.

A member of the circle next placed a tumbler half full of water upon the table and a slip of paper between the medium's lips. The light was then extinguished. After a few moments singing by the circle the light was ordered, and the tumbler was found empty, with no trace of the water upon the table or the floor, the medium being still tied as last described, his feet within the pencil lines, and the paper between his lips dry. Again the light was put out, and again relighted in a few moments, when the medium was found untied. This closed the second series of experiments.

Mrs. Spence, now sat near the medium, and facing him. A gentleman then sat between the two, so as to place his right foot upon Mrs. Spence's feet, his right hand upon the medium's head, and his left hand upon Mrs. Spence's head. The medium then grasped the gentleman's right arm with both hands, each hand grasping at separate places, while Mrs. Spence grasped the gentleman's left arm in the same way. The light was put out, and after a short interval, it was again struck up, when the parties were observed to be still in the relative position just described.

The gentleman then stated, that neither the medium's nor Mrs. Spence's hands had been removed from his arms; yet, while the light was out, he distinctly felt the fingers of a hand playing upon his face, pull his nose, slap him upon the cheek, making a noise that was heard by the rest of the circle; also that he was repeatedly tapped over the head with the violin, making a noise that was perceptible to all present.

Another gentleman then took the first gentleman's place, and he also stated that he was handled and struck in the same way; and so each member of the circle, taking, in turn, the position just described, testified to having been touched, handled and struck about the face and head, by what seemed to be a hand, and sometimes also by the violin; all, however, while the light was extinguished, but while the medium's hands and feet and also Mrs. Spence's were secured as described. This closed the third series of experiments, in all of which, as well as in those first two series, we are satisfied that the manifestations were not produced either by Mr. Fay or by any member of the circle.

Yours truly,

Charles Patridge, R. T. Hallock, Mrs. Sarah P. Clark, Mrs. Mary S. Hallock, Mrs. Amanda, M. Spence, Miss

Alla Britt, William Blondel, William P. Coles, W. B. Hallock, B. Franklin Clark, Peyton Spence.

New York, May 3, 1861."

OBSERVATION: We don't deny the possibility of all these things and we have no reason to doubt the honorableness of the countersigners, despite the fact that we don't know them. However, we stand behind our thoughts given in our last issue regarding the two articles about the mysterious drawings and the exploitation of Spiritism. Some say that such exploitation does not shock public opinion in America and that they find it very natural that mediums may seek compensation. That is understandable in a country where time is money. That will not preclude us from saying what we have already said in another article: that the absolute altruism is an even better guarantor than all physical precautions.

If our texts have contributed to cast discredit upon the self-serving mediumship in France and elsewhere we believe that this is not the least service done to serious Spiritism. These general thoughts are not absolutely directed to Mr. Fay whose position before the public we ignore.

November 1861
Spiritism in America
Fragments translated from the English by
Ms. Clémence Guérin[6]

Spiritism in America accounts for a number of very renowned individuals who have assessed its scope from the beginning and have seen in it something more than merely manifestations. Among them we find Judge Edmonds, from New York, whose writings on these important subjects are much appreciated and still not known enough in Europe due to lack of translation.

---

6 Large brochure, 18-in, price 1 franc. Dentu Edition, Palais Royal, Galerie D'Orléans.

We are grateful to Ms. Guérin for giving us an idea about these writings based on some fragments that were published in her brochure, and at the same time we regret the fact that she had not finished the work in a more comprehensive translation. She also adds some not less remarkable extracts from Dr. Hare, of Philadelphia; who was also one of the first to make a statement of faith regarding the new revelations. Ms. Guérin lived in America for a long time where she saw the production and development of the first manifestations, and she is one of those sincere and conscientious Spiritists, judging everything with calmness, coolly and without enthusiasm. We have the honor of having met her in person and we gladly give her here the much deserved testimony of our profound admiration. By the fragment of her preface transcribed below one can see that our opinion is thoroughly justified.

"Like the Americans, we have a deep faith and radiant hope that this Doctrine, so eminently based on charity (not alms, but love), is the one that will regenerate and pacify the world. Never before has fraternal solidarity been so clearly demonstrated and more seductively. The spirits come to reassure us, help us, teach us and indicate to us the best use of our faculties, in seeing to the future; the spirits are evidently so much altruistic that one cannot hear them without feeling the need to imitate them; without reaching out to others, willing to share the benefits that we have so generously been given. The human being does so with much more good will when he finally understands that it is the price to pay for his own advancement and that he only enjoys the merit of his own actions in the great book of God, aiming at the moral or material well-being of his brothers and sisters. What the spirits are successfully at doing right now has already been attempted several times on Earth by noble hearts and courageous souls but who were and still are unknown or ridiculed. People now have an idea about their devotion but this only happens when they disappear and then have a chance of being assessed with impartiality. That

is why God allows them to continue their work after what we call death. It is an opportunity to repeat from Andrew Jackson Davis: 'Brethren, fear Not: for Error is mortal and cannot live; Truth is immortal and cannot die!'

Clémence Guérin"

The passage below from Judge Edmonds will show how accurately he had foreseen the consequences of Spiritism. One not forget that he wrote it in 1854, a time when Spiritism was new in America as it was in Europe.

"Others will evaluate if my deductions are true or false. My objective will be achieved if by speaking about the effects produced in my spirit by these revelations I give rise to the desire in some people to also investigate them, and thus bring new light into the study of these phenomena since up until now the most vehement adversaries, who shout against the imposture, these are also the most obstinate in their resolution to not hear or read anything about this subject; the most adamant to remain in complete ignorance about the nature of the facts. People that uphold the reputation of knowledge, if not Science, are not ashamed for providing explanations that satisfy no one, based on superficial observations carried out with such a light-heartedness that would make a young student blush. However, this new power connected to the human being is not something indifferent and it will undoubtedly have a considerable influence on good or evil."

"And we can already see that since its origin just five years ago the spiritualist idea propagated with a speed that the Christian religion did not equal in a hundred years. It does not seek deserted places, is not surrounded by mysteries, but comes openly to people inviting a detailed examination, not demanding a blind faith but recommending the exercise of reason and free judgment at all times."

"We saw that the attack of the philosophers could not shake a single believer; that the sarcasm of the press and the anathemas of the Academy are equally powerless to stop its progress and, most

importantly, we can already attest its moralizing influence. The true believer always becomes a wise and better person because it was demonstrated to him or her that the existence after death has been positively proven. All of those, who have carried out serious and sincere investigations on the subject, have found irrefutable proof. How could it be otherwise? Here you have an intelligence that speaks to us every day. It is a friend (In general, Americans begin by talking to relatives or friends.) He proves his identity by a thousand circumstances, leaving no room for doubts and through recollections that only he may have. He speaks about the consequences of the Earthly life and paints the future life with such rational colors giving an assurance that he is telling the truth since it agrees with our innermost ideas of divinity and the duties imposed on us."

"Our loved ones are not separated from us after death and they are often close to us, we are helped and consoled through the hope of a certain reunion. How many times have I heard them, through me or through others! How many desolated people I have seen calmed by the gentle certainty that the beloved relative 'brought back by the bonds of love is around them, whispering in their ear, gazing upon their soul, conversing with their spirit?'

"Consequently, death is stripped from the entourage of mysterious and undefined terrors with which it was surrounded by those who expect more from the degrading passion of fear than from the noble feeling of love. Note that in passing, regardless of the variations in the teachings of the new philosophy, every disciple agrees that death is not a threatening specter but a natural phenomenon; a transition to an existence that is free from a thousand ailments of the material life and from the barriers that confine them to a single planet, the spirit may travel the infinity of the worlds and set flight to the regions where the Glory of God is actually visible."

"It is equally demonstrated that our most secret thoughts are known by those who were our loved ones and that continue to watch over us. It is in vain to try to escape this terrible inquisition

by its benevolence. One cannot doubt it even if they wanted too. Often I was stunned and shuddered at the unforeseen but irrefutable revelation that our most intimate thoughts and conscience may be examined by the very ones from whom we wanted to hide our weaknesses."

"Isn't that a healthy obstacle against having bad thoughts, criminal acts that in their majority are carried out because the guilty mind was assured by these words: 'Nobody will know...'? If anything can confirm this truth so terrifying to some, it is the memory that all of us experience after a good deed, even when it was a secret: an inner satisfaction that cannot be compared to anything else. They know well because the left hand ignores what the right hand did. It is then rational to assume that if our friends may congratulate us, they can also reproach us; if they see our meritorious actions they also see our mistakes."

"By this we do not hesitate in attributing the incontestable and uncontested fact that there is not a single believer that has not become a better person. Our future destiny depends on our conduct. Not on our adhesion to this doctrine or other particular religious sect, but on our submission to this great precept: LOVE GOD AND THY NEIGHBOR... We must not postpone our conversion. We have to work towards our own salvation, not later but now; not tomorrow but today."

"There is nothing more reassuring, more strengthening to a virtuous soul in the trials and vicissitudes of this life than the thorough assurance that one's future happiness depends on one's actions, actions that can be guided. On the other hand, the wicked, the vicious, the cruel, the selfish and especially the selfish will endure self and mutual torments, torments that are worse than a material hell, something that even the most deranged imagination could ever imagine."

Allan Kardec[7]

---

7   Paris, Typography Carion, Rue de Bonaparte 64.

Year 1862

SPECIAL AMERICAN EDITION

February 1862
Reincarnation in America

People are frequently surprised by the fact that reincarnation has not been taught in America and the nonbelievers do not let the opportunity go and accuse the Spirits of contradiction. We will not repeat here the explanations that were given to us and that we have published about it. We will just remind our readers that the Spirits showed their usual caution with this.

They wanted Spiritism to appear in a country that provided absolute freedom of opinion. Their essential point was to have the principle accepted and consequently they did not want to be disturbed by anything else. The same did not happen with respect to the consequences, particularly the reincarnation that would have clashed against the prejudices of slavery and color. The idea that a black person could become white, a white person could have been black, and a master could have been a slave seemed so monstrous that it would be sufficient to have all the rest rejected. Hence, the Spirits preferred to momentarily sacrifice the accessory to the main part and have always told us that a unity would be later established about that point as others as well. In fact this is what is happening. We heard from several citizens of that country that such doctrine now finds many followers there; that certain Spirits have now confirmed it, after having previously given some insight into the matter. Here is what Mr. Fleury Lacroix, an American citizen, sent us from Montreal, Canada:

"… The issue of reincarnation that you were first wanting to openly promote has taken us by surprise over here. We are now reconciled with that extension of your thoughts. Everything has become clear through this new clarity and we now see our future much more broadened in our eternal journey. However, it seemed absurd to us, as I said in the beginning. We deny today and believe tomorrow – such is humanity. Fortunate are the ones who wish

to learn because they see light; unfortunate are the others who remain in darkness."

Thus, it was logic and the power of reasoning that led them to that doctrine since it gave them the only key capable of solving problems, which up until then were unsolvable. Our honorable correspondent, however, is mistaken with respect to one important point by attributing to us the initiative of that doctrine that he calls the daughter of our thoughts. It is an undeserved honor since the reincarnation was taught to others by the Spirits and before the publication of *The Spirits' Book*.

Furthermore, the principle was clearly exposed in several other prior works, besides ours, at the time of the turning tables, like among others in the *Heavens and Earth* by Jean Reynaud and in the fascinating little book by Mr. Louis Jourdan entitled Prayers of Ludovico, published in 1849, not to mention that this principle was professed by the Druids who have not certainly learned from us.[8] When it was revealed to us, we were caught by surprise and received it with hesitation and mistrust. We even fought against it for some time until evidence demonstrated it to us. Hence, we accepted rather invented it and that is very different.

This answers the objection of one of our subscribers from Antwerp, Mr. Salgues, a confessed adversary of reincarnation, who seems to think that both the Spirits and mediums that teach it suffer our influence and since the Spirits that communicate with him teach the opposite. In fact Mr. Salgues makes special allegations against reincarnation that we will one day examine in detail. While we wait we observe a fact: the number of believers grow incessantly whereas the number of opponents decreases. If that is the result of our influence it must be huge since it extends to America, Asia, Africa and Oceania. If the

---

8 See the April 1858 issue of The Spiritist Review, article about Spiritism among the Druids and the Triads.

contrary opinion is the truth how come it does not prevail? Is the mistake more powerful than the truth?

February 1862
New American Mediums in Paris

T he American mediums are now in larger numbers and strength than those of the old continent, in the case of physical manifestations. Their reputation is well established in that area, particularly after Mr. Home who seems to promise prodigies of his own.

For many people Mr. Squire was simply called American medium, a charlatan that used to travel around towns and fairs some years ago, making presentations and announcing himself as an American medium, although he was perfectly French. We have just received two others now that only have the names of mediums and that we would not have mentioned here since their art is strange to our matters but their arrival was announced with a fuss and caused a certain sensation, given the nature of their pretensions. To the benefit of our readers and to avoid been charged with partiality, we fully transcribe below the text of their flyer that has inundated Paris.

"Fun in the Parisian salons – novelty, nothing more than novelty!!! Family soirees and private sessions given by the American Mediums, Mr. C. Edwards Girroodd, from Kingstown, Lake Ontario, and Mrs. Julia Girroodd, nicknamed by the English and American press as the Graceful Sensitive."

"An album of more than 200 pages containing compliments from the greatest dignitaries of France, from nobility, magistrates, army and literature, as well as from sixteen archbishops and bishops of France and from a large number of ecclesiasts of elevated distinction, available to persons who would like to throw soirees but who wish to carry out a previous examination of the good taste, richness and novelty of the experiences."

"Mr. and Mrs. Girroodd, the only one to carry out the experiences in France, spent only three months in Paris and provided forty two sessions in the top notch salons of Paris and in the Tuileries on May 12th 1861, as well as in the house of several members of the Imperial family."

"They immediately placed the experiences well above anything that they could have seen before as entertainment in get-togethers. Their magic tricks, contrary to the habit of Mr. Physicists, does not required any preparation or special arrangement and the artists easily operate amidst a circle of attentive spectators unafraid of seeing their illusion destroyed."

"The magic acts are only a tiny part of their varied talents. The world of the Spirits obey their commandments: Visions – Ecstasy – Fascination – Magnetism – Electro Biology – Rapping Spirits – Spiritism, etc. everything that science and charlatanism invented and that stupefy the believers of our days, even giving them a robust faith in everything that is nothing but charlatanism, where are inadvertently accomplices. In one word, Mr. and Mrs. Girroodd after having shown themselves as witches – but high-class witches – wise like Merlin, the enchanter, will demonstrate the secrets of their science, if needed."

"Christian faith can only gain from the clear demonstration that everything that was not taught by that faith is nothing but brilliant charlatanism. For the little meetings or soirees with the children Mr. Girroodd hired the most skilled Physicists from the capital city and a ventriloquist nicknamed The Man of the Talking Dolls who will give sessions at a reduced price."

As one can see the couple's pretension is not but that of destroying Spiritism posing as the defenders of the Christian faith that no doubt is much surprised by finding deception at its service. This, however, can expand a certain clientele.

They pretend to be mediums and are not careful enough to omit the title of Americans, an indispensable passport, like the names ended by the letter "i" to the musicians, and that to demonstrate that mediums do not exist since – they say – they can be reproduced with support of some skills, mechanics and some particular means that allow them to do everything done by the mediums.

All this demonstrates one thing: the fact that everything can be imitated. Illusion is a matter of skill set. Nevertheless, just because something can be imitated does not mean that it does not exist? If trickery imitated lucid somnambulism in order to deceive, should one conclude that there is no somnambulist? Fake copies of Raphael were made and taken by originals. Was Raphael an illusion? Mr. Robert-Houdin changes water into wine; he takes thousands of objects out from a hat and fills up a big box with them. Does it harm the miracle of Cana and the multiplication of bread? He does better, however, than just transforming water into wine for he produces half a dozen of delicious liqueurs from a single bottle.

All physical manifestations are wonderfully prone to imitation and these are the ones exploited by the charlatans. They do much better than the Spirits, particularly in the case of trans-portation, since these are produced at will and whenever they wish to do so, something that cannot be done by the Spirits or the best mediums.

As a matter of fact, justice must be done to that gentleman and that lady once they do not intend to deceive the public. They do not pretend to be what they are not. They present themselves as skillful conjurers and that is more commend-able than those who pretend to be mediums and even more respectable than the true mediums that add trickery to reality in order to produce more effects and win over competition. It is true that openness is eventually politically correct but trying to demonstrate through deception that the mediums are conjurers has a touch of novelty that will be abundantly compensated by curiosity.

As we said, their skills cannot prejudge the reality of the phenomena. Far from causing any harm, it will be of great utility. To begin, it will be another trumpet calling people's attention to Spiritism, people who have not heard about it. As with every criticism, they will be willing to see the pros and cons. The result of the comparison is undisputable. An even greater utility is that of preventing fraud and subterfuge from the part of false mediums; demonstrating the possibility of imitation to those who risk ruining its credit.

If there could be something wrong found in their skills set so as to easily identify if they were true mediums. Unfortunately they are on the other side of the Atlantic and hence we do not have the privilege of observing Mr. and Mrs. Girroodd. If we can one day attend one of their sessions it will be a pleasure to inform our readers.

When we say that everything can be imitated we must take exception for the really normal conditions in which the Spiritist manifestations can be produced, hence one can say that every phenomenon that does not respect those conditions, must be considered suspicious. Now, in order to carefully judge something one needs to study it. The intelligent manifestations themselves are not exempt from charlatanism. There are some manifestations that, given their own nature and the circumstances in which they are produced, challenge the most established skill of imitation. As an example, the evocation of the dead who reveal details of their private lives that are unknown to the mediums and to the audience. Add to this the fact that these are dissertations, consisting of many pages, written in a surge, spotless, speedily, with eloquence, profundity, wisdom and sublimity of thoughts about certain subjects, are beyond the capacity, knowledge and understanding of the medium.

To achieve such a result one would need an omnipotent individual. Well, these type of individuals are rare and do not give public showings. This is, however, what is seen every day not by a privileged individual but by thousands of individuals of all ages, sex, social condition, education and whose honorableness and absolute altruism are the best guarantee of honesty since charlatanism does not give anything for free. If Mr. and Mrs. Girroodd wanted to accept any challenge from us it would be on these terms; we would gladly leave the physical manifestations to them.

NOTE: A supposedly well informed person tell us that the name Edwards Girroodd must be translated into Edouard Girod and Kingstown, Lake Ontario replaced by Saint-Flour, Cantal (France).

March 1862
Spiritist Teachings and Dissertations
Reincarnation

The Hague envoy – medium M. le Baron de Kock

"The doctrine of reincarnation is an incontestable truth and if someone wants to only think of God's love, wisdom and justice then one cannot admit any other doctrine. It is true that the following words are found in the sacred books: "Man will be rewarded for his works, after death"; But one does not pay enough attention to the endless quotes that tell you that it is completely unacceptable that modern man is punished for the mistakes and crimes of those who lived before Christ. I cannot go back to so many examples and demonstrations given by those who believe in reincarnation. You can do that yourself and the good Spirits will help you with that, and it will be a pleasant task for you. You can add this to the message I gave you and to those I will give you if God allows. Rest assured of God's love for humanity; God wants the happiness of His children but the only way for them to one day reach such supreme happiness is thoroughly in the successive reincarnations.

I already told you that what Kardec wrote about that fallen angels is the greatest truth. The majority of the Spirits that populate your world have always done so. If they are the same who return for so many centuries is that few have earned the reward promised by God.

Christ said: "This race will be destroyed, and soon the prophecy will be fulfilled". If you believe in a God of love and justice, how can we admit that a person who currently lives and even who has lived for eighteen centuries could be guilty of Christ's death without admitting reincarnation? Yes, the feeling of love for God, the punishments and rewards of the future life, and the idea of reincarnation are innate in humans for centuries. Look into all stories, see the writings of the sages of antiquity, and you will be convinced that this doctrine has always been accepted by everyone who understood the righteousness of God. Now you understand the meaning of our Earth, and how the time has come for the prophecies of Christ to be fulfilled.

I am so sorry that you only find a few people that think like us. Your countrymen only think of greatness, money and name. They reject everything that can preclude bad passions. May that not withdraw your courage, though! Work for your own happiness and for the good of those who may renounce to their mistakes. Persevere on your work; always have God and Jesus in your thoughts and the heavenly beatitude will be your reward.

If the problem is examined without prejudiced, taking into account the existence of humankind in the several conditions of society and conciliate that existence with God's love, wisdom and justice and every doubt with respect to reincarnation will disappear.

In fact, how can one reconcile that justice and love with a single existence where everyone is born in different social positions; where one is rich and great while the other is poor and miserable; where one enjoys good health while the other endures diseases of all sorts? Here joy and pleasure; sadness and pain elsewhere; a well-developed intelligence in some while it is just above the brute in others. How to believe in a God that is all love and who made beings condemned to idiotism and madness for life? Who allows children at the spring of their lives to be taken away from the kind warmth of their parents?

I even dare ask if one can attribute love, wisdom and justice to God before those individuals that are immersed in ignorance and barbarism when compared to the civilized nations where there is the rule of law and order and where art and sciences are cherished.

It is not enough to say: "That is how God has established things in His wisdom". No, the wisdom of God that is love before anything else must become clear for the understanding of everyone. The dogma of reincarnation explains everything. That dogma given by God Himself cannot oppose the precepts found in the Sacred Scriptures. Far for that, the dogma explains the principles from which moral betterment and perfection stems out. The future revealed by Christ is in agreement with the infinite attributes of God. Jesus said: "All humans are not only children of God: they are also brothers and sisters of the same family". Now, those expressions must be well understood.

Will a worldly father give to some children what is denied to others? Will he throw one of them into the abyss of misery while the other is cumulated with wealth, distinction and dignity? Besides, since the love of God is infinite it cannot be compared to that of a man for his children. Since the different positions of people have a cause and since that cause is based on the principle of love, wisdom, benevolence and justice of God then their only explanation must be found in the doctrine of reincarnation.

God created all Spirits equal, simple, innocent, without vices or virtues, but with the free-will of controlling their actions according to an instinct named conscience, an instinct that gives them the ability to distinguish between good and bad. Each spirit is destined to reach the highest perfection after God and Jesus. In order to achieve that the spirit must acquire the whole knowledge through the study of all sciences; be initiated in all truths and purify through the practice of all virtues. Well, since these superior qualities cannot be acquired in a single existence they all have to live several lives in order to acquire the multiple degrees of knowledge.

Human life is the school of the spiritual perfection in a series of tests. That is why the spirit must know all social conditions and do what it takes to carry out the divine will in all of them. Wealth and power as poverty and humbleness are tests; pain, idiotism, madness, etc. are punishments for some bad deed of a previous life. As with the free will, the individual may pass or fail the test to which one is submitted. In the first case the reward will not be long: it consists on a progression towards the spiritual perfecting. In the second case the spirit is punished through the reparation in a new life of a lost opportunity in the preceding existence from which the spirit was not able to take advantage. Before the incarnation the Spirits wander in the celestial spheres: the good ones enjoying happiness, the bad ones regretting, victimized by the pain of being abandoned by God. However, keeping the memory of the past allow the Spirits to remember their breaches of God's laws and God allows them to choose their tests and conditions in a new existence, and that explains why we frequently find noble feelings and advanced understanding in the lower echelons of society while sometimes finding ignoble inclinations and brute Spirits in superior classes.

Can we speak of injustice when a person that has badly employed her life can repair her faults in a new existence and get to the final destination? Wouldn't injustice be in the immediate condemnation and without a possible way back? The Bible speaks of eternal penalties but that should not really apply to a single life, so sad and short, that instant, that blink of an eye when compared to eternity.

Many people ask why God would have hidden this dogma for such a long time, a dogma whose knowledge is useful to our happiness. Would God have loved humanity less than in our time?

The love of God is for the whole eternity. In order to enlighten us He sent wise people, prophets and the Savior Jesus Christ. Isn't that a proof of an infinite love? However, how has humanity received that love? Have they improved?

Jesus said: "I still have many things to say to you, but you cannot bear them now"[9]. If we take the Sacred Scriptures in their intellectual meaning we will find many citations that seem to indicate that the spirit must experience several lives before reaching the end. Besides, do not we find the same ideas about reincarnation in the works of old philosophers?

The world has progressed significantly in the material aspect, in sciences and social institutions but from a moral point of view it is still crawling behind. Humanity still ignores God's law and no longer listen to Jesus' words; that is why God gives them as a last resort and as a means of getting to know the principles of the eternal happiness the direct communication with the Spirits and the teaching of the principle of reincarnation, words that are plentiful of consolation and that illuminate the darkness of the dogmas of so many different religions.

Hands on! May the search be carried out with love and confidence! Read without prejudices; think of everything that God has done to humanity since the creation of the world and you will be confirmed in the faith that reincarnation is a sacred and divine truth."

9 John 16:12 [USSF]

OBSERVATION: We did not have the honor of knowing Mr. Baron de Kock. This communication that agree
with all principles of Spiritism is not the product of any
personal influence.

April 1862
Consequences of the Doctrine of Reincarnation on the Propagation of Spiritism

" The fast propagation of Spiritism is a fact that nobody
can deny. When something propagates it means that it
is convenient. If Spiritism propagates it is then convenient.
There are several reasons for that. The first one, and without
contradiction, is the moral satisfaction given to those who
understand and practice it. But even the strength associated
to this very reason is partially influenced by the principle of
reincarnation. That is what we shall try to demonstrate.

Every wise person will always give some worthwhile thought
to a future life after death. Who on Earth would give more
importance to a few days than to a number of years? Even
more: during the first stage of life we work, endure and suffer
all kinds of restrictions so that, in the second stage, one can
enjoy some rest and wellbeing.

If we are so careful with respect to some undefined years
isn't that rational to be even more so with respect to our life
beyond the grave, whose duration is unlimited? Why is that
the majority of people work more for the volatile present than
for the endless future? Fact is that we believe in the reality of
the present and doubt the future. Now, one can only doubt
what is not understood. Once the future is understood the
issue is over.

Even to the eyes of those taught by common beliefs and
who are better convinced about a future life it presents itself

so vaguely that faith is not always enough to sink in that idea which is more characteristically hypothetical than reality.

Spiritism comes to destroy such uncertainty by the testimony of those who have already lived and by proofs that are in a way material.

Every religion is necessarily based on a future life and all dogmas forcibly converge to that unique end. That is the objective of the practice of those dogmas and one's faith in them is directly proportional to the efficacy that one attributes to them in order to achieve that goal.

The theory of a future life is then the keystone of every religious doctrine. If that theory has a faulty foundation; if it opens up the door to serious objections; if it is contradictory; if the impossibility of certain parts is demonstrated, everything else falls apart. To begin with doubt is established. It is then followed by absolute denial and the dogmas are dragged down with the wreckage of faith. Some thought that banning the discussion and prescribing blind faith, as a virtue would avoid the danger.

The imposition of a blind faith, however, is ignorance of the times in which we. Willing or not people think; examine by the force of things; people want to know how and why. The development of sciences and technology shows the best terrains where one must set foot on. That is why we probe that one where we shall walk after death. If we do not find it sturdy enough, that is logical and rational, we leave it alone. However much they try they will not be able to neutralize this tendency that is inherent to the moral and intellectual development of humanity. According to some this is good. According to others, this is bad. Regardless of how we see it we must accommodate to the situation since there is no way out.

The need to be aware and understand things goes from the material to moral life. Future life is certainly not the most touchable thing like a railroad or a steam engine but it can be understood through reasoning. If the train of thoughts employed to understand it does not satisfy reason then premises and conclusions are abandoned. If we question those who deny a future life and they will all say that they were lead to disbelief by the very picture that was shown to them with its entourage of devils and flames and endless suffering.

All moral, psychological and metaphysical questions are more or less connected to the issue of the future. It thus follows that this issue depends in a way on the rationality of the philosophical and religious doctrines. Spiritism in turn does not come as a religious but as a philosophical doctrine, bringing its doctrine founded on the fact of the manifestations. It does not impose itself; it does not demand a blind faith; it meddles with people and say: "Analyze, compare and judge. If you find anything better than what I give you than take it."

Spiritism does not say: "I come to destroy the basis of religion and replace it by a new cult". It does say: "I do not address the believers and those who are happy with their beliefs, but those who have abandoned their ranks in disbelief and for the fact that you did not know how or could not retain. I come to provide a rational interpretation to the truths that they reject, leading them to accept those truths. The number of souls that I take out of the swamp of disbelief is the proof that I can do it."

Listen to them when they all say: "Had I been taught these things since my childhood and I would have never doubted. Now I believe because I understand."

Should they be sent away for the fact that they do not accept the letter, but the spirit; the form but the principle? You are free to do so. If you feel that it is a duty to your conscience, nobody will violate that. However, I wouldn't say that this is a lesser mistake. I say more: it is unwise.

As we said, future life is the essential objective of the moral life. Moral life has no foundation without future life. The triumph of Spiritism is precisely in the way it presents future life. Besides the proofs given by Spiritism, the picture that is painted is so clear, so logical and according to the goodness and to the justice of God that people say: "Yes, that is how it must be; that is how I had envisaged it and if I did not believe it the reason is the fact that I was taught differently."

However, what is it that gives such a power to the theory of the future? What is it that makes it so attractive? We say that it is its inflexible logic that solves all the up until now unsolvable issues and that it is owned to the principle of the plurality of the existences. In fact, remove that principle and there will immediately appear thousands of problems, each more unsolvable than the next. In every step of the way we are faced by many objections. Such objections were not raised in the past because nobody thought about them. Now that the child has grown up the adult wants an in-depth understanding of things; the path must be clear; people probe and balance the actual value of the arguments and if these do not satisfy their reason, leaving them in darkness and uncertainty, they are then rejected until something better shows up.

The plurality of the existences is a key that opens new horizons; that gives meaning to many things that were misunderstood; that explains what was inexplicable. It conciliates the events of life with God's justice and benevolence. That is why those who had doubted such justice and goodness now acknowledge the hand of Providence where it was ignored before.

In fact without reincarnation what can explain the innate ideas? How to justify cretinism, mental diseases, and barbarism side by side with the genius and civilization? The deep misery of some next door to the happiness of others? The premature deaths and so many other things?

From a religious point of view certain dogmas like the original sin, the fallen angels, the eternity of the penalties, the resurrection of flesh, etc. find in that principle a rational interpretation that leads to its acceptance, even by those who used to reject the word.

To summarize, modern civilization wants to understand. The principle of reincarnation illuminates what was obscure before. That is why we say that such a principle is one of the reasons that favor people to welcome Spiritism.

One could argue that reincarnation is not necessary to believe in Spirits and their manifestation. A proof of that is the fact that there are believers who do not admit such principle. It is true. We do not say that one cannot be a good Spiritist without that. We are not among those who throw stones at people that do not think like us. The only thing we say is that they have not discussed all the problems raised by the system of a single life, otherwise they would have recognized the impossibility of finding a solution to all of them.

In the beginning the idea of the plurality of the existences was received with surprise and mistrust. People then gradually familiarized with that as they recognized the impossibility of solving many difficulties without that principle, difficulties raised by psychology and future life.

There is one thing for sure. This system gains terrain every day while the other loses it. The adversaries of reincarnation these days in France – we speak of those who have studied the Spiritist science – count on a tiny number when compared to those who accept it. Even in America where they are in larger numbers for the reasons that we gave in our previous issue, such a principle begins to popularize. From that one can conclude that it is not far the day when there will be no disagreement about this point.

April 1862
Spiritist Dissertations
The Martyrs of Spiritism

Regarding the questions about the miracles of Spiritism that had been proposed to us and that we discussed in our last issue there is also the following question:

"The martyrs have sealed the truth of Christianity with their blood. Where are the martyrs of Spiritism?"

You are very kin on having the Spiritists burning at the stake or thrown to feed the beasts! This leads to the assumption that you would be willing to do so in case it was possible. You want to sneak Spiritism in on the same level as a religion! Notice, however, that has never been the intent; that it has never pretended to rival Christianity, on the contrary naming itself the child of Christianity; that it combats its cruelest enemies: atheism and materialism.

We attest once more that Spiritism is a philosophy that rests on the fundamental basis of every religion and on the moral of Christ. If Spiritism renegaded Christianity it would be betraying itself, it would be suicidal. It is the enemies of Spiritism that present it as a new sect, giving it priests and a high clergy. They shall scream so many times that Spiritism is a religion that we will end up believing that it is.

Do martyrs require a religion to exist? Haven't sciences, arts and other disciplines had their own martyrs side by side with their discoveries? When the Spiritists are pointed at as condemned people, people to be avoided, the scum of society, when ignorance is incited against us to the point of subtracting people means of subsistence in the absence of better arguments, aren't they helping to create martyrs?

Nice victory had them triumphed! However, the seed has been sown and blossoms are everywhere. If uprooted in one place it flourishes in a hundred others. You must then try to harvest the whole planet but allow the Spirits to speak, those on a mission to answer the questions.

I

You have asked for miracles. Today you demand martyrs. You already have the martyrs of Spiritism. Get inside the homes and you will see them. You ask for persecuted. Open the heart of those eager followers of the new idea who fight against the prejudices of the world and even and frequently that of the family! Ah, their broken hearts expand and embrace a father, a mother, a brother or a wife only to find the reciprocity of sarcasm, disdain and neglect. The martyrs of Spiritism are those who hear these insulting words every step of the way: mad, senseless, lunatic! And for a long time they shall have to withstand such attacks of incredulity and other even more bitter sufferings.

Nonetheless, their reward will be beautiful as Christ has prepared a delightful place for the martyrs of Christianity and the one prepared to the martyrs of Spiritism is even more wonderful. The martyrs of the infancy of Christianity marched resigned and courageously to the martyrdom expecting to suffer for only a few days or hours, aspiring for death as the only barrier that separated them from a celestial life.

The martyrs of Spiritism must not even seek death. They must suffer for as much time as it pleases God to have them on Earth and dare not judge themselves worthy of the pure celestial pleasures as soon as they leave life. They pray and wait whispering words of peace, love and forgiveness to those who did them harm, waiting for new incarnations in which they will be able to atone previous faults.

Spiritism will be erected as a superb temple. The first steps will be difficult to climb. Nevertheless, once the first steps are covered the good Spirits will help to overcome the others up until the simple and righteous place that leads to God. Go, go children and preach Spiritism!

Martyrs are requested. You are the first ones marked by God for you have been duly appointed and you are treated as mad and senseless because of the truth! I tell you, however, that the time of light is near when there will no longer be persecuted and persecutors. You shall all be brothers and sisters and the same feast will unite oppressed and oppressors!

Saint Augustine, medium Mr. E. Vézy

II

The progress of times has replaced physical torture by the martyrdom of conception and the birth of new ideas, daughters of the past and mothers of the future. When Christ came to destroy the barbarian costume of sacrifices; when he came to proclaim equality and fraternity between the simple clothes of the worker and the noble outfit the altars were still smoking the blood of the immolated victims; the slaves trembled before the caprices of their master and the peoples ignored God's justice, forgetting his greatness.

In such a low moral state Jesus' words would have been impotent and neglected by the crowds if they had not been screamed out of his injuries and become sensitive by the ulcers of the martyrs. In order to be accomplished the mysterious law of similarities required that the blood gushed out of the ideas was rescued by the bloodshed of brutality. Today peaceful people ignore physical torture. It is only their intellectual being that suffers in the struggle between the traditions of the past and the aspiration to new horizons.

Who could describe the anguishes of the present generation, its pungent doubts, uncertainties, impotence and its extreme lassitude? Uneasy presentiments of superior worlds, pains ignored by the material antiquity that only suffered when unable to enjoy; pains that are the modern torture and which will transform in martyrs those inspired by the Spiritist revelation who will believe but will not be believed; they shall speak and be censored; they will march and be repelled.

Have no fear. Your enemies themselves prepare you an award that shall be the more beautiful the more they have sowed in your way.

Lazarus, medium Mrs. Costel

III

As you correctly say, the beliefs have always had martyrs, at all times. However, one must say that fanaticism was frequently on both sides and almost always there was bloodshed. Today, thanks to the moderators of passions, to the philosophers or even with this philosophy that began with the writers of the eighteenth century, fanaticism put its fire out and laid down its weapon down. In our days one can hardly imagine the spade of Mohamed; the gallows of the Middle Ages; the burning at the stake and tortures of all kinds, in the same one that magicians and witches are no longer invoked.

Other times other costumes says a wise proverb. The word costume here is very elastic, as you see, and according to its Latin etiology it means habits, way of life. Well, it is not our costume to cover ourselves in cilice in our century, as it is not our habit to pray hidden in the tombs and dissimulate our prayers to the powerful and to the magistrates of Paris.

Hence Spiritism will not see the axe swinging and the fire devouring its followers. The blow of ideas, books, commentaries, eclecticism and theology now abates people but St. Bartholomew shall not happen again.

Certainly there could be victims in the underdeveloped world but the civilized nations will only see the struggle of ideas and ridicule.

Therefore, no more axes, bundled wood and the boiling oil but to be aware of the badly understood spirit of Voltaire. That is the executioner. It is necessary to prevent it but not defy it. It laughs instead of threatening; it casts ridicule instead of blasphemy and its sufferings are the tortures of the spirit that succumbs when braced by modern sarcasm.

Nonetheless, not displeasing the little Voltaire of our days, the youth will easily understand these three magic words: freedom, equality and fraternity.

As for the sectaries these are more terrible because they are always the same, regardless of time and anything else. They can sometimes do harm but they are lame, masked, old and grumpy. Now you who met the source of youth and whose soul flourish and renew, have no fear for they shall lose to their own fanaticism.

Lamennais, medium Mr. A. Didier

April 1862
Bibliography
Andrew Jackson Davis

We call the attention of our readers again to the interesting brochure by Ms. Clemence Guerin, entitled: Biographic essay by Andrew Jackson Davis, one of the main spiritualist writers of the United States of America. Ledoyen Edition, price 1 franc.

Allan Kardec

November 1862
Medication prescribed by the Spirits

The title above will provoke laughter on the nonbelievers. Never mind! They laughed at many other things that did not preclude them from being acknowledged as true. The good Spirits care about the suffering of humanity. Hence it does not come as a surprise the fact that they try to bring us relief and they have proved on many occasions that they can do it when they are elevated enough to have the necessary knowledge since they can see what the human eyes cannot and foresee what people cannot foresee.

The medication in question was given to Ms. Ermance Dufaux[10] in the circumstances below – she sent us the formula with an authorization to have it published in favor of others who could benefit from that. One of her relatives who had died long ago had brought it from America. This prescription was a balm that was highly efficient in the treatment of ulcers and wounds. With his death the prescription that was not passed on to anybody was then lost.

Ms. Dufaux was affected by an old and serious illness in her leg that had been resisted to all sorts of treatments. Tired of the uselessness of so many medicines one day she enquired her protector spirit if would there be any possible cure in her case.

— Yes, he said. Use the balm of your uncle.

— But you know that the prescription was lost.

— The spirit then dictated the following:

— "*Saffron, 20 centigrams, cumin 4g, yellow wax 31-32g, oil of sweet almond 1 spoon. Melt the wax and then add the oil; add the saffron and the cumin in a little cloth bag and simmer for ten minutes. Spread the ointment on a piece of cloth and cover the wound. Renovate the procedure every day. Before applying the medication, it is necessary to wash the wounded area with mallow water or another refreshing lotion.*"

Ms. Dufaux followed the instructions and very soon thereafter her leg was healed and, since then there has been no other incident. A lady that does laundry works for her was also cured of a similar illness. A worker that was injured by a shrapnel from a sickle and that penetrated deeply in his leg presented significant swelling to the point of being told that

10   Medium who wrote the story of Joan of Arc.

there would be the need for the leg to be amputated. After the application of the same ointment the swelling disappeared and the piece of metal was removed from the wound. The man totally recovered and was back to work in eight days. When applied onto abscessed boils, it suppurates and heals in a very short time. It acts by removing the morbid principles from the ulcer then healing it by allowing the removal of slivers when applicable, like a speck of bone, wood, etc. It seems also to be good to herpes and all affections of the skin in general. Its composition, as seen above, is very simple, easy and inoffensive. One can then try it without worries.

November 1862
Spiritist dissertations
Foundations of the social order

Lyon, September 16th, 1862 – medium Mr. Émile V…

Note: This communication was obtained in a private session presided by Mr. Allan Kardec

Here you are gathered to see Spiritism at its foundation, to face this idea and to appreciate the huge waves of love that overwhelm those who get to know it. Spiritism is moral progress; it is the elevation of the spirit on the way to God. Progress is fraternity in its infancy for complete fraternity as imaginable by the spirit is perfection. Pure fraternity is a perfume from above, an emanation from the infinite, an atom of celestial intelligence; it is the basis of all moral institutions and the only means of achieving a sustainable social order and producing the effects worthy of the cause that you have embraced. Hence, be brothers and sisters in humanity if you want the seeds sowed among you to develop and become the tree that you seek. Union is the sovereign power that comes to Earth and fraternity is the sympathy in the union, it is the poetry, the enchantment, the positive ideal.

You must be united to be strong and be strong to cast the foundations of an institution that is solely based on the truth, the so-much admirable, touching, simple and sublime truth. When divided, the strength disappears. When united, it becomes stronger.

When we think about the individual progress of each person, about the love and charity that comes out of each heart the power shall be much greater. Under the sublime breeze of this ineffable breath, family bonds become stronger and the social links so vaguely defined become bolder, get closer and establish a unique stream with all kinds of thoughts, wishes and objectives.

What can you see without fraternity? Selfishness and greed. Each one with their own objective; each one concerned with themselves only; each marching separately and everyone inexorably dragged to the abyss in which human dreams have been drowning for centuries. With union there is only one objective since there is only one thought, one desire and one heart. Hence, my friends, unite and that is what the voice of our spiritual world repeats incessantly. Unite and you shall reach the objective more rapidly.

It is particularly in this entirely sympathetic meeting that you must make the irrevocable resolution of being united by a thought common to every Spiritist on Earth to offer the tribute of your acknowledgement to the one who has opened to you the path to the supreme good; the one who brought happiness to your minds, joy to your hearts and faith to your souls. Your acknowledgment is your present reward. Therefore do not refuse that and make your offer in one voice only walking the first step of true fraternity.

Léon de Muriane, protector spirit.

OBSERVATION: This name is totally unknown, even to the medium. This demonstrates that to be an elevated spirit it is unnecessary to have one's name inscribed in the archives of history and that there are many unknown Spirits among those who communicate.

Year 1863
SPECIAL AMERICAN EDITION

Jan 1863
Barbarism in civilization
Horrific torture of a black man

A letter from New York, dated November 5th and addressed to the Gazette des Tribunaux, contains the following horrible details of an appalling tragedy that took place in Dalton, Caroline County in Maryland:

"A young black man was recently arrested under the accusation of lewd behavior against a young white female. Severe charges were filed against him. The young woman declared to recognize him perfectly well. The accused was taken to Dalton jail. He was there for a few hours when a huge and enraged crowd screaming for vengeance demanded to have the poor black man delivered to them. Authorities uselessly tried to stop the violent crowd. Their words in favor of law and justice were met by the mobs' boos.

The masses, whose number was on the rise, started to stone the jail. Gun shots were fired against law enforcement but did not reach them. Once they realized that it was impossible to resist any longer the jail's doors were open. The crowd shouted and invaded the place furiously. The prisoner was dragged out to a town's central square amidst screams of rage and supplication by the victim.

A jury was immediately staged, the facts examined, and the prisoner found guilty and condemned to death by hanging. The prisoner was promptly hung on a tree by a rope that was tied around his neck. While the black man's body contorted following the convulsions of death he was also victimized by the insults and violence by the crowd. Blindfolded by rage and vengeance the mob did not wait for the stillness of the body, parading the streets of Dalton with their despicable trophy. Man, women and even children applauded the injuries imposed on the poor black man's body. The mob's anger, however, would not stop there. After parading around the streets of Dalton in every direction they stopped in front of a black church. A huge bonfire was pitched only to noisily receive and devour the flesh and the mutilated parts of the body."

Such report gave rise to the following question raised at the Parisian Society on November 28th, 1862:

"One can understand isolated and individual examples of anger among civilized people. Spiritism explains this when describing inferior Spirits. In such cases, these individuals have displayed their evilness during their whole life. What is more difficult to understand is a whole population that has given proofs of intelligence and superiority and even given demonstrations of humanitarian feelings on other occasions, who profess a religion of kindness and peace, be taken by such a blood thirsty vertigo, showing a savage rage to the point of being fed by the torture of the victim. This is a moral issue we ask the Spirits to kindly enlighten us."

Parisian Society, November 28th, 1862
Medium Mr. A. De B…

Bloodshed in countries towards human progress is a rain of curse. It is near the time when the wrath of a just God shall fall upon those regions where such abominations take place like the one you have just heard.

In vain we want to hide ourselves from the consequences that are inevitably established; in vain we want to mitigate the importance of the crime. The crime is awful by itself not less by the intention that led to the execution with such horrendous refinements of cruelty, with such a bestial fury. The interest! Human interest! Sensual pleasures, the satisfactions of pride and vanity were once again the drives as on other occasions, and the same causes will give rise to similar effects, causes, in turn, of the effects of the heavenly wrath that has threatened so many iniquities.

Do you believe that there is only real progress with technology and all resources and arts that tend to sooth the rigors of material life and increase the insatiable need of pleasure? No, that is not what summarizes the progress of the Spirits, which are only temporarily human and who should only give human things the secondary interest they deserve.

The development of the heart, the illumination of conscience; the diffusion of the sense of universal solidarity of beings and that of brotherhood among humans are the only authentic milestones that distinguish a people marching towards general progress. These are the only traces that identify the most advanced nation. But those who still harbor feelings of exclusive pride and only see such a portion of humanity as a serving race, cut to obey and suffer, those will no doubt experience the nullity of their claims and the weight of Heavens' vengeance.

Your father, V. De B...

February 1863
Sermons against Spiritism

A letter from Lyon, dated December 7th, 1862 contains the following passage verbally confirmed to us by a witness:

"We had the presence here of the Bishop of Texas, USA, who preached on Tuesday, 8th December, at 8pm at Saint-Nizier Church, before an auditorium of about two thousand people and a large number of Spiritists. Ah! He does not seem to be well informed about our Doctrine. One can judge from this summary: *The Spiritists do not admit hell or prayer in church. They lock themselves in their bedrooms and pray to God there, who knows which prayers! There are only two types of Spirits: the perfect ones and the thieves; the murderers and the villains...I come from America where these blasphemies began. I can assure you, though, that for a couple of years now nobody is involved with these things there any more...I was told here in this famous city of Lyon that there was a lot of Spiritists here. This cannot be true. I don't believe it. I am positive, brothers and sisters, that there isn't a single medium among you for behold the Spirits do not accept marriage or baptism and every Spiritist separates from their spouses, etc.*

"Those few statements give you an idea of the rest. What would the preacher say if he had known that a quarter of the audience was made-up of Spiritists? As for his eloquence, I can only say this: at certain times he was frantic; he seemed to have lost his train of thoughts and did not know what he wanted to say. If I was not afraid of using an disrespectful expression, I would say that he floundered. I do believe that he was led to say such absurd things by some Spirits and, so much so, that I assure you that we even forgot that we were in a sacred place. Everybody was laughing. Some of his followers came outside to observe the effect produced by the sermon but may not have been very happy since each person laughed and said what they thought. Several of his friends deplored his attitude and understood that he had not achieved his objective. This is what happened in the next session. A lady that was sitting by a very kind Spiritist friend of mine asked: *What is this Spiritism and these mediums that people speak so much about it and what are these men so furious about? She thought about the explanation and said: - Ah! When I get home I will try to acquire the books and understand.*

"I assure you that it is thanks to some of these sermons that there are so many Spiritists in Lyon. Keep in mind that only three years ago we were only a few hundred when I wrote to you about a wrathful sermon against the Doctrine that had excellent results. I surmised that a few sermons more like this one and, in a year, the number of followers would double. Well, as predicted, the number is a hundred-fold today thanks also to the false attacks from the press.

Everybody, including the simple worker on his simple outfit has more common sense than one may think when something is attacked with such emphasis. As a result, these individuals wanted to investigate the merits of Spiritism themselves. They soon recognized the untruths of certain allegations that denoted ignorance or malevolence, discrediting the critics and bringing more followers to Spiritism instead of keeping them away. The same happens, we hope, to the Bishop of Texas whose greatest mistake was to say that *'every Spiritist is separated from their wives'*, when we have here before our eyes many couples that were separated before and that found union and concord in Spiritism.

Everyone naturally tells themselves that if the adversaries of Spiritism give it false teachings but yet the results demonstrated by the facts and by the reading of the books show the opposite, there is then nothing to confirm the truthfulness of their criticism. I do believe that if the Spiritists of Lyon were not afraid of showing a lack of respect for the Bishop of Texas, they would have sent him and thank you letter. Spiritism, however, makes us charitable, even to our enemies."

Another letter from a witness contains the following passage:

"The preacher from Saint-Nizier assumed that Spiritism had had its time in the USA and that for two years now nobody talks about it. Hence in his opinion it was a matter of fashion. The phenomena had no consistence and did not deserve further studies. He sought to see and saw nothing. However, he added that the new doctrine was destructive to the links of family, to the property and to the constitution of Society thus he denounced it to the authorities.

The adversaries expected a more shocking effect and not a simple denial presented in such a ridiculous way as the people are not oblivious to what happens in town, to the march of progress, and to the nature of the manifestations. The issue resumed on Sunday 14th in Saint-Jean, this time handled a little bit better. The preacher of Saint-Nizier denied the phenomena. In Saint-Jean he acknowledged them and said:

People hear raps on the walls, in the air, mysterious voices; in reality these are from Spirits but which Spirits? They cannot be good since the good ones are kind and obedient to God's orders which prohibits the evocation of Spirits. Hence the ones that come can only be the bad ones.

There was about three thousand people in Saint-Jean. Among those at least three hundred will seek the discovery. What will certainly contribute to the thoughts of honest and intelligent people that made the audience are the singular statements of the preacher – I say that out of education. *Spiritism*, he said, *comes to destroy the family, to degrade women, to preach suicide, adultery and abortion, to promote communism and dissolve society.*

He then invited the parishioners who eventually had Spiritist books to come forward and give it to them so that they could be burnt like St. Paul did to the heretic books in Ephesus. I don't know if those gentlemen will find people eager enough to take their money and empty our bookshelves. Some Spiritists were furious; the majority rejoiced for understanding that it was a great day.

Hence, from the top of the second cathedra of France they have just proclaimed that the phenomena are true. The whole issue then is reduced to knowing that if these are good or bad Spirits and if the bad ones have God's permission to come."

The preacher of Saint-Jean affirms that it can only be the bad ones. He modified a little bit the solution.

We got a letter from Angouleme last Thursday, December 5th telling us that a preacher expressed himself in this way during his sermon: *"We all knew that the Spirits could be evoked and since long ago but it can only be done by the Church. Other people are not allowed to try to correspond with them by material means. To me it is a heresy."* The effect it had on people was entirely contrary to the expected.

Thus, it is obvious that the good ones and the bad ones can communicate since if only the bad ones had such a power it is not reasonable that only the Church had the privilege of calling them.

We doubt that two sermons given in Bordeaux in the last October had served better to the cause of our antagonists. Below follows the analysis done by one listener. The Spiritists will be able to see if under this disguise they recognize their Doctrine and if the arguments opposed to them can smother their faith. As for ourselves, we repeat what we have already said somewhere else: While Spiritism is not attacked with better weapons it has nothing to fear.

"I will always regret", says the narrator, "the fact that I missed the first of these sermons at Margaux Chapel, on October 15th last, if I am not mistaken. According to what I heard from trustworthy witnesses the thesis that was developed was the following: *The Spirits may communicate with people. The good ones only communicate with the Church. All those who manifest outside Church are bad because there is no salvation outside Church. The mediums are miserable people who established a pact with the devil obtaining from him manifestations of all sorts at the price of their soul, extraordinary if not miraculous manifestations.*"

I give below other citations still stranger than that one. Since I did not hear them I suspect these statements could be exaggerated.

"The following Sunday, October 19th I was lucky enough to hear the sermon below. I tried to learn the name of the preacher and I was told that it was Father Lapeyre.

Father Lapeyre offered insights to his critics of *The Spirits' Book*. In order to do so, he certainly tried to raise issues from this remarkable piece of work. I will restrain myself to point out the arguments that were more shocking to me, choosing to stay below the truth rather than assigning to our adversary something that he might not have said or that I might have misunderstood.

According to Father Lapeyre, *The Spirits' Book* preaches communism; sharing of assets; divorce; equality among all peoples and in particular between men and women; equality between man and his God since man aspires nothing less than become similar to Jesus Christ taken by a pride that was the loss of the angels. The book drags people to materialism and to sensual pleasures since the works of progress may take place without God's support and despite God, through the effect of this force that wishes the betterment of everything gradually, promoting the metempsychosis, this insanity of antiquity, etc. Then moving on to the speed with which the new ideas propagate he attests horrified how skillful and smart the devil is, by bringing them about; how well and artfully he was able to elaborate them to strongly vibrate in the perverted hearts of this century of incredulity and heresies. He then states: *This century loves freedom so much and offer him free examination, freedom of choice, freedom of conscience! This century loves equality so much and shows him human beings at the same level of God! This century loves light so much and with a movement of the hand tears off the veil that hid the sacred mysteries.*

He then attacks the subject of the eternal penalties and gave magnificent pieces of oratory embedded in emotions. *Believe me, my dear friends; believe me when I tell you where the imprudence of these new philosophers taken them thinking that they have dismantled the sacred religion of Jesus Christ before the weight of their deceptive assertions. Ah! Disgraceful! There is no hell, no purgatory, they say! To them no more blessed relationships connecting the living ones to the souls of those who they lost. No more the sacred sacrifice of the mass! Why would they celebrate it? Wouldn't their souls purify by themselves without any work and just by the efficacy of that irresistible force that attracts them to perfection non-stop? And do you know who the authorities are that come to proclaim these impious doctrines stamped on their foreheads by the indelible sign of hell that they wanted to annihilate? Ah! Brothers! These are the strongest columns of the Church: St. Paul, St. Augustine, St. Luke, St. Vincent de Paul, Bossuet, Fénelon, Lamennais, and all renowned men, true saints that fought for the establishment of the unmovable truth in their time and upon which the Church built its foundations, coming now to declare that their Spirits, detached from matter and more clairvoyant realized that their former opinions were wrong and that people should believe in the opposite.*

Then, moving on to a question that the author of a Letter from a Catholic addressed to a Spirit to know if one commits heresy by practicing Spiritism, the preacher adds: *Here is the answer, brothers: It is curious that despite the devil's astuteness and skills he always shows his claws by the name of the Spirit that gave this answer. I will tell you in a little while.*

"This is followed by the citation of that answer that goes like this: *Are you in agreement with all truths of the Church that empower you in the good that boosts the love for God in your soul and the devotion to your brothers? Yes; hence, you are a Catholic. He then adds: - Signed... Zenon... Zenon! A Greek philosopher, a pagan, an idolater that from the flames of hell where he burns for over twenty centuries comes to tell us that one can be a Catholic and not believe in that very hell that tortures him, waiting for all those who do not die humble and obedient in the heart of the Church... But senseless and blind you are! With all your philosophy you will not have but this proof, this only proof that the doctrine that you promote comes from the devil and that shall be a thousand times enough!*

After a lengthy explanation about this and the exclusive privileges of the Church to expel the devil, he adds: *Insensible people that have fun by talking to the Spirits pretending to have any influence upon them! Have no fear like with the one mentioned by St. Luke these rapping and noisy Spirits – and they are very well classified my brothers – will not ask you: Who are you? Who are you to disturb us? Do you really believe that we are going to submit to your sacrilegious caprices? And that taking the tables and chairs that you turn around wouldn't they take you over like the son of Sceva, bringing pain upon you to the point that you have to run away, harmed and naked, too late to acknowledge the true abomination that is like playing with the dead?*

What is left to be done before such positive facts that shout at us? What to do? Ah dear brothers! Watch out and be careful not to be contaminated. Repel all the outrageous attempts of evil to drag you along towards the abyss. However, it is too late for such recommendations. Evilness has progressed rapidly. Those infamous books dictated by the prince of darkness to attract a multitude of ignorant people to his kingdom have spread out so much that like in Ephesus in former times if we added the price of those that circulate in Bordeaux alone it would amount to more than fifty thousand silver denarius (170,000 francs in our currency, repeating the citation made elsewhere in the sermon). I would not be surprised if among the believers that hear me now there wouldn't be some who have already fallen for the reading of those books. We can only say to these ones: Hurry up! Approach the tribunal of penitence. Hurry up! Come and open your hearts to the spiritual guides. Full of benevolence and kindness and always following the magnificent example of Paul we shall forgive you right away. As with Paul, however, forgiveness shall not be given to you if you do not bring us those books of sorcery that have almost destroyed you. What shall we do to those books, dear brothers? Yes, what shall we do? As St. Paul did we will build a mountain at the main square and we ourselves will set them on fire."

Just a quick observation about this sermon: the author is mistaken about the date and perhaps, like a new Epimenides of Knossos, he has been asleep since the fourteenth century. Another fact that sticks out is the rapid development of Spiritism. The enemies of another school also attest it in despair, such is the great love that they have for human reason.

The Moniteur de Moselle on November 7th, 1862 reads: *"Spiritism makes dangerous progress. It invades the upper, middle and lower classes of society. Magistrates, doctors, serious people also fall in that trap."*

This statement is repeatedly found in the majority of current critics. In the presence of such a positive fact it was necessary to come from the middle of Texas and enter an auditorium with over a thousand Spiritists who have not been practicing for two years. Then, why such a rage if Spiritism is dead and buried? At least Father Lepeyre has no illusions. Given his horror he even exaggerates the extension of the supposed evil for he estimates the Spiritist books in Bordeaux alone to be worth a fortune. Nevertheless, he acknowledges that the idea has a great power and nobody will say that we exaggerate when we speak of the fast progress of Spiritism. Some may attribute this to the devil fighting in a struggle against God, others may say that this is a fit of insanity invading all social classes so much so that the circle of shewed people narrows down continuously to the point that it will soon count on only a few, Others may deplore these things and each one from their own standpoint, asking themselves: *What is going to be, God?* It is their own right. The result is that Spiritism wins over every barrier that is placed on its path. Hence, if it is insanity then soon there will only be mad people on Earth. It is a well-known proverb. If it is the work of the devil, then soon there will only be deranged people around and if those only speak in the name of God cannot stop them then the devil is stronger than God.

The Spiritists are more respectful of the Divinity. They do not believe that there is someone capable of fighting God on a level plan and even more to defeat God. Otherwise the roles would be upside-down and the devil would be the true lord of the universe. The Spiritists say that since God is sovereign there is no sharing there and that nothing happens without

God's permission. Consequently, if Spiritism propagates with a lightning speed it does so by the will of God regardless. Since God is sovereignly fair and good he must not expect that his creatures will be lost or allow them to be tempted knowing from his foresight that they will succumb and precipitate in the never ending torments.

The dilemma still stands now. It is submitted to everybody's conscience and the conclusion is up to the future. If we mention all that there is to demonstrate the position of the adversaries of Spiritism when attacking it. In fact, one does need many excuses to criticize Spiritism by preaching the breakdown of family, adultery, abortion, communism and the destruction of social order. Do we need to rebuff those things? No. It is simply enough to guide them to Spiritism and its teachings, something that is done all over the place.

Who would believe that we preach communism after the lessons given about the speech published in full in the report of our journey in 1862? Who could see an incitement to anarchy in the same brochure, page 58: *"In any case the Spiritists must be the first ones to give the example of submission to the law in case they are drawn."*

Proposing such things in a distant region where Spiritism was totally unknown, where there was no means of controlling that could produce some effect. But saying it from the top of the cathedra of truth, amidst a whole population of Spiritists who permanently contradict it by their teachings and examples, that is real inability and one cannot help it but say that someone must be deluded to the point of not understanding that such speech can only serve the cause of Spiritism. It would be a mistake, however, to believe that that opinion is shared by the entire clergy. Much to the contrary, there are several priests who don't think that way and we even know some who deplore such deviations that more harmful to religion than to the Spiritist Doctrine. These are personal opinions that do not make law. A proof of the personal appreciations is their contradiction. While one says that all Spirits that manifest are necessarily bad for disobeying God, another one acknowledges that some are good and some are bad but only the good ones go to Church and the bad ones to the masses. One accuses Spiritism of degrading women, another one criticizes it for elevating women to the same level as men. One pretends that Spiritism "drags people to materialism and sensuality" and the other, Mr. Cure of Marouzeau, recognizes that it destroys materialism.

Father Marouzeau says the following in his brochure: *"In reality, according to the followers of the communications from beyond the grave, it would be the deliberate intention of the clergy to fight Spiritism at any price. Let us suppose that the clergy has so little intelligence and common sense and a stupid mind? Why believe that the Church that has given so much demonstration of prudence, wisdom and high intelligence to discern the truth from the false at all times would be now incapable of understanding the interest of its children? Why condemning without listening to the Church. If the Church refuses to hold your flag it means that it is not its flag whose colors are essentially hostile; fact is that side by side with the good that you do by fighting materialism the Church sees a real danger to souls and Society."* And in another passage: *"Let us conclude from all that that Spiritism must limit itself to fighting materialism and giving people tangible proofs of immortality by means of well-established manifestations from beyond the grave."*

An essential point that results from all of this is the fact that all those gentlemen are in agreement with respect to the reality of the manifestations. The only difference is in the way each one appreciates them. As a matter of fact, denying them would be the same as denying the truth of the Scriptures and the facts themselves upon which the dogmas are founded.

As for the way people look at the thing, it is already possible to verify how the unity is established and how public opinion manifests itself, an opinion that also has its power of vetoing. Another fact sticks out: the Spiritist Doctrine touches profoundly the masses; while some see in the doctrine a terrible ghost others see an angel of consolation and freedom and a new era of moral progress to humanity.

Since we mentioned Father Marouzeau's brochure we may perhaps be asked why we have not responded to that once it was addressed to us, personally. The reason may be found in the report of our journey we have traveled to refute these assertions. When we discuss a subject, we do so from the general point of view, abstracting from personalities that to our eyes are just individuals attached to their principles.

We shall talk about Mr. Marouzeau and others when the time is right to discuss the ensemble of objections. It was necessary to wait until each one would speak – bragging or not – in order to appreciate the strength of the opposition. Individual and particular responses would have been premature and repeated incessantly.

Mr. Marouzeau's brochure was a rifle shot. Our apologies for placing him in the category of the rifleman but his Christian modesty shall not be offended.

Protected by a number of shields it seemed convenient to us to let them unload their guns, even the heavy ones, like the one that has just arrived, so that we could assess their power. Well, up until now we cannot lament the clearings in our ranks. On the contrary, their shots ricocheted. On another hand it was not less useful to allow the situation develop and people should appreciate the fact that over the last two years instead of worsening the general state of things we have gathered new strengths every day. Hence we will respond when we understand that the time is right. So far, there has been no waste of time for we have gained terrain constantly and the adversaries themselves facilitate our job. All we have to do is to let them act.

March 1863
Spiritist photography

The *Courrier du Bas-Rhin* from Saturday, January 3rd, 1863 (German part) brings the following article under the title "Spectral Photography":

"The Americans that do not advance in many things are certainly ahead of us with respect to the art of photography and the evocation of spirts. Nowadays in Boston dead people are not only called back by mediums but also photographed. The wonderful discovery is attributed to a Mr. William Mumler from that town. He describes it himself: *I have been experimenting for some time now in my laboratory with a new photographic device taking pictures of myself. Suddenly I felt a pressure on my right arm and a lethargic sensation took over my whole body. What a surprise when I saw my picture with the image of a second person by my side, the image of nobody else but my dead cousin? The similarity of the image leaves no doubt in the minds of those who knew the lady.* As a result and since then Mr. Mumler not only provide his customers with mediumistic sessions but also takes pictures of the evoked souls. These are generally somehow faded and foggy and the outlines difficult to recognize but that does not preclude the enlightened people of Boston from testifying in favor of their authenticity. Who would believe that the spectral images would come so soon?"

In case it was real such a discovery would certainly have huge consequences and would be one of the most remarkable facts of manifestations. However, our recommendation is to take it with careful reservation. The Americans that surpassed us in so many things, in the words of the author of the article, have also moved ahead in the field of deception.

To those who know the properties of the perispirit at first sight, this does not seem materially impossible. So many extraordinary things are discovered that this does not seem to be a big surprise. The Spirits announced manifestations of a new kind, even more remarkable than the ones that we have already seen. This one would then and undoubtedly fit that category. However and once more until there is a more authentic verification than a report from a newspaper it is sensible to remain in doubt. If it is true it will then become common; while we wait, it is then necessary to avoid believing in all wonderful stories that the enemies of Spiritism rejoice in spreading to bring ridicule upon the doctrine and those who accept it so easily. Besides, one does need to observe things more carefully before attrib- uting every unexplained and remarkable phenomenon to the Spirits. A detailed analysis shows, in the majority of the cases, an entirely material cause that had not been observed yet. It is our clear recommendation in The Mediums' Book. As a support to what we have just said and with respect to the Spiritist photography we mention the following article extracted from the La Patrie on February 23 rd , 1863. It helped us to forewarn ourselves against hastily judgment.

"A young Lord, bearing one of the oldest and illustrious names of the high chamber, whose love for the art of photography brings to that field great and joyful successes, had just lost his beloved sister. Heartbroken and profoundly sad he left his equipment behind, left England and went on a long journey around the continent, only returning to his almost noble Lancashire home about four years later. Unsurprisingly his desperation moved from an acute to a chronic condition, that is, it had not changed in intensity but only in violence, gradually transforming into resignation. When those in suffering seek consolation they first address God, then work. Later on, the young lord returned to the laboratory and his photographic gadgets. In a kind of transaction with his pain he thought of starting the imagery by the chapel where the remains

of his sister were buried. He got the negative and prepared the plate to be exposed to light in order to obtain the revealed picture. When he looked at the plate he almost passed out. The interior of the chapel appeared very clearly but the head of the dead young lady was showing vaguely at the not well lit part of the photography. Her beautiful and kind traces were nicely distinguished including details of her dress. Minor details of the chapel could be seen through the fabric of her dress.

The lord's initial reaction was to believe in an apparition. He soon nodded his head in sadness. He remembered that some years back he had photographed his sister using the same plate. Since the image was poor he had erased it, now realizing that he might not have done it properly for the outlines of his sister were mixing with the new image impressed upon the plate. Some artists in England exploit this bizarre photographic technique: they produce and sell double images whose assembly leads to strange or funny effects. Among other things one can see the ruins of a castle on top of its park, façade and pavilions as they should have looked like before their destruction. They also prepare the montage of old people through which one can see how they looked like in their good old days when they were young."

March 1863
Varieties
American Mediums, Mr. and Mrs. Girroodd,

(. . .) An article published in the *Monde Illustré* about the supposed American mediums Mr. and Mrs. Girroodd have also motivated many requests for information. We have nothing to add to what we have already said in the February 1862 issue of *The Spiritist Review* other that the fact that we saw them in person and that one can also see with Robert Houdin things that are not less unexplainable when the intricacies are not understood. No Spiritist or magnetizer can take those things seriously or waste any time in serious discussions about them when they know the normal conditions in which the phenomena take place.

Certain inept adversaries wanted to exploit those skills against the Spiritist phenomena by saying that if they can be imitated it means that they do not exist and that every medium is a skillful swindler, starting by Mr. Home. They fail to observe that they provide ammunition to discredit themselves for the same argumentation may be used against the majority of the miracles.

Without pointing out the illogical aspect of that conclusion and without discussing the phenomena again we say that the difference between the swindlers and the mediums is the difference between the profit and the selflessness, between imitation and reality, between an artificial flower and a real one. Furthermore, we cannot preclude a con man from pretending to be a medium or a physicist. It is not up to us to defend any exploitation of that kind. Let us leave it up to the critics.

April 1863
Spiritism and the Spirits by Mr. Flammarion
Extracted from the Revue Française

Mr. Flammarion, author of the brochure about the *"Plurality of the inhabited worlds"* that we mentioned in our January issue, has just published a first and very interesting article in the February 1863 edition of the Revue Française whose initial part is given below. The work requested by the periodical is an important and widely spread literary summary of the principles of Spiritism. The extension of the work almost gives it the title of a special publication for it has nothing less than 23 large format pages (in-8). Up to a certain point the author thought adequate to abstract from his personal opinion about the subject and stay in a kind of neutral terrain, limiting himself to an impartial presentation of the facts thus giving the reader a total freedom of appreciation.

Here is how he begins:

"In a century where metaphysics has fallen from its pedestal; in which the religious idea wanted to stay away from any dogma and special cult; in which philosophy itself changed its way of thinking in order to connect to the positivism of experimental science, a spiritualist philosophy was offered to humanity who received it. That philosophy proposed a symbol of belief that was adopted by its people. It showed them a new avenue leading to unexplored regions and they followed it and there you have it a doctrine based on the manifestations of invisible creatures, standing from its birth above ordinary things, universally propagating amongst peoples of the new as well as the old world. What is then this powerful breath that has led so many thinking heads to gaze the same point in the skies?

Simple utopia or a real science; fantastic deception or a profound truth fact is that it is before our eyes and it shows us the flag of Spiritism uniting a large number of champions around it, today counting on millions of followers. And that prodigious number was formed in the short span of ten years.

The event is then before us: it is an undeniable fact. Now, whatever the frivolity or importance of this fact wouldn't that be useful to study it on its own merit so that we can establish if it has the right to live among the children of progress; if its path is parallel to the movement of progressive ideas or if it would not tend, as some people pretend, to make us march backwards towards deprecated beliefs unworthy of consideration.

And considering that in order to analyze any subject we must know it very well, before anything else, so that we do not expose ourselves to erroneous appreciations, we will gradually examine the points upon which Spiritism rests; about the basis that sustains the theory of its teachings and in short what this science is about. Notice that we are talking about facts and not speculative systems and adventurous opinions for, irrespective of how wonderful the analyzed matter, Spiritism is purely and simply based on the observation of facts. If that were not the case, if it were only another religious sect, a new philosophical school, we are certain that the event would lose a lot of its importance that and that serious people of the present time, in its majority disciples of the "Baconian" method, would not have wasted their time examining a pure matter of theory.

Many utopias were written in the book of human weakness so that we no longer have to take into account the dreams daily proposed by exalted brains.

Let us now and without a hidden agenda discuss this doctrinaire science that a lot of good and bad things have been said about but without studying it sufficiently. In this current work, we begin by its modern history — since Spiritism has its old history — bringing about the successive phenomena that have definitely established the doctrine. Following the natural order of things, we will examine the effects before going back to the causes."

It is then followed by the first manifestations in America, its introduction in Europe and its conversion to a philosophical doctrine.

Year 1864

SPECIAL AMERICAN EDITION

April 1864
Authority of the Spiritist Doctrine
Universal control of the teachings of the Spirits[11]

We have already discussed this subject in the last issue of the Review regarding a special article (The perfection of the created beings) but that is so important and has consequences of such a magnitude for the future of Spiritism that we find appropriate to analyze it in a more comprehensive way.

If the Spiritist Doctrine were a purely human conception its only guarantee would be the enlightenment of the person that had conceived it. Now, nobody here could have the founded pretension of knowing the absolute truth by themselves. If the Spirits that revealed it had manifested to a single person nothing could guarantee its origin and everyone would have to believe in the word of that person that would have received their teachings. Admitting a total honesty from the part of the person that would have received it the most it could do would be to convince those that lived in the same environment. That person could find followers but never attract everybody.

God wanted the revelation to get to us through the fastest and most authentic path. That is why the Spirits were assigned with the mission of taking it from one pole to the next, manifesting everywhere, not given anybody in particular the exclusive privilege of hearing their words. A person may be mistaken, may deceive others but that could happen when millions of people see and hear the same thing. That is a guarantee to each and every one.

Besides, people can get rid of a single person but cannot do that to the crowds; books can be burnt but the Spirits cannot. Even if all books were destroyed the source of the Doctrine would not be extinguished because it is not on Earth, it shoots

---

11 This text is item II of the introduction of *The Gospel According to Spiritism*. [USSF]

everywhere and everybody can enjoy it. In the absence of people to spread it there will be Spirits that reach everyone and that cannot be reached themselves.

In actual fact it is the Spirits that make the propaganda supported by a large number of mediums that are solicited everywhere. If they had a single interpreter, however skilled that medium might be, Spiritism would be hardly known. That single interpreter, irrespective of the social class, would have felt prevention from all sides and from many people. That medium would not have been accepted by all nations, whereas communicating to all peoples and everywhere, to all sects and parties, the Spirits are accepted by all.

Spiritism has no nationality. It is indifferent to any particular cult; it is not imposed by any social class since everybody may receive communications from relatives and friends from beyond the grave. That was necessary so that Spiritism would invite humanity to fraternity. If not placed in a neutral ground it would have created dissension rather than peace.

Such universality of the teaching of the Spirits constitutes the strength of Spiritism. That is also the cause of its fast propagation while the voice of a single person, even with the support of the press, would have taken centuries to get to everyone's ears and there we have thousands of voices that are simultaneously heard in all corners of the globe, proclaiming the same principles, transmitting them to the most ignorant as to the wisest person so that nobody may be left behind. It is an advantage not enjoyed by any doctrine so far. If then Spiritism is a truth it fears no bad will of people nor the moral revolutions or the physical cataclysms of the world because none of these things can affect the Spirits.

But that is not the only advantage that results from such an exceptional position. Spiritism finds in that a powerful guarantee against the divisions that could result from the ambition of certain persons or the contradictions of certain Spirits. Such contradictions are undoubtedly an embarrassment but that carries in itself the very remedy to the disease.

It is well-known that the Spirits, by force of the differences in their capacities, are individually far from holding the whole truth; that not all of them are given the right to have access to certain mysteries; that their knowledge is proportional to their purity; that vulgar Spirits don't know better than people on Earth and even less than certain persons; that among them as with ourselves there are presumptuous and pseudo-wise Spirits that believe to know what they actually don't; systematic one that take their ideas by the truth; finally that the Spirits of a more elevated order, those that are completely dematerialized are the only ones that are free from the earthly prejudices.

But it is also well-known that deceiving Spirits have issues in hiding under borrowed names to have their utopias accepted. From that it follows that anything that is beyond exclusively moral teachings the revelations that anyone can receive have an individual character, without authenticity; that they must be considered as personal opinion from this or that Spirit, and that it would be unwise to accept them and lightheartedly promote them as absolute truths.

The first control is undoubtedly that of reason to which one has to submit, without exception, everything that comes from the Spirits. Any theory that is manifestly in contradiction with common sense, with a rigorous logic and with positive facts that are available, however respectable the signature may be, must be rejected. However, such a control is incomplete in many cases due to the lack of knowledge of certain persons and the tendency that many have of making their own judgement as the only referee of truth. In such cases, what do the people that do not have much confidence in themselves? Follow the opinion of the majority and that opinion is their guide. That is how it must be with respect to the teaching of the Spirits, and these means we are taught by the Spirits themselves.

Therefore, the best control is the agreement in the teaching of the Spirits but that still does need to occur in certain conditions. The least safe is when a medium question several Spirits about a doubtful point. It is obvious that if the medium is enduring a case of obsession and dealing with the same deceiving Spirit that Spirit can tell her the same thing with different names.

Also, the conformity obtained by multiple mediums of the same center is not enough because they may be suffering the same influence. *The only serious guarantee that there exist is in the agreement between spontaneous revelations made through mediums of a large number of mediums that are strange to one another and in several regions.*

It must be understood that we are not talking about communications of secondary interest here but those that attain to the principles of the Spiritist Doctrine. Experience demonstrates that when a new principle must be learned it is taught spontaneously and in several points at the same time and in identical conditions if not in its form at least in its meaning.

Hence, if a Spirit wishes to propose an eccentric, based on its own ideas and not necessarily true, we can rest assured that such a system will remain inside a limited circle and will fall down before the unanimous instructions given everywhere, as we have already seen in several examples. It is that unanimity that knocked down all partial systems that were born at the origin of Spiritism when each one explained the phenomena their own way and before the laws that govern the relationships between the visible and invisible world were known.

Such is the foundation on which we base ourselves when formulating a principle of the Doctrine. We do not promote it as true because it agrees with our own ideas; we do not put ourselves in place of absolute judges of the supreme truth and we do not tell anyway: "Believe in this because we say so." Our opinion, before our own eyes, is nothing more than a personal opinion that can be either right or wrong and by the simple fact that we are not more infallible than anybody else. In addition, it is not because a principle was taught to us that we believe it to be true but because it received the endorsement of the general agreement. That universal agreement is a guarantee to the future unity of Spiritism and it will nullify all contradictory theories. That is where the criteria of truth will be sought in the future.

The success achieved by both *The Spirits' Book* and *The Mediums' Book* is that every person may receive directly from the Spirits the confirmation of their teachings. If they were contradicted by the Spirits from all sides, they would have found long ago the same destiny of the fantastic ideas. Even the support of press would not have saved the wreckage whilst they propagated rapidly without that very support because they counted on the Spirits and they compensated by far the bad will of people. That is how it is going to be with every idea that may come from the Spirits or from the human beings that cannot endure the trial of that control that is not in anyone's hands.

Let us then suppose that certain Spirits decide to dictate a book with a given title and whose principles are contrary to those. Let us even imagine that with the objective of discrediting Spiritism apocryphal messages were produced by malevolence. What would be the influence of such texts if they are disproved by the Spirits everywhere? One should count on the adhesion of the latter ones before releasing a system in their name. The distance between a system of a single Spirit and that of all Spirits is like the distance between the unity and infinite.

What can all the arguments of the detractors about the general opinion do when millions of friendly voices from space and in all corners of the globe and within the cell of each family come to contradict them? Hasn't experience already confirmed the theory about that? What happened to all publications that pretended to have come to annihilate Spiritism? Which one has even precluded its march? Up until now this subject had not been faced by that viewpoint, undoubtedly one of the most serious. Each one of them counted on themselves but not on the Spirits.

A capital truth stems from that: Any person that wanted to oppose the flow of the established and endorsed ideas could well cause a small local and momentarily disturbance but never dominate the whole both in the present as well as in the future.

It also points out the fact that instructions given by the Spirits about issues that are not clarified yet could not become law while isolated ideas and that consequently must be only accepted with the highest reservation and as informational.

Hence the need to be very careful when publishing them and, if judged appropriate, their publication still needs to show these works as individual contributions. That is the confirmation that must be expected before a principle is presented as an absolute truth. This is also to prevent the contributor of being accused of lightheartedness or unthoughtful belief.

The superior Spirits proceed with extreme wisdom in their revelations. They only gradually touch the great questions of Spiritism. They introduce new concepts as our intelligence levels become more capable of understanding the truths at a more elevated level. That is why they have not said everything from the beginning and even today they did not say everything, never yielding to the impatience of hasty persons that are ready to harvest the fruit before it's time. It would then be useless to try to precipitate the time scheduled by Providence for each thing because the really serious Spirits would refuse to help. The lighthearted Spirits though give little importance to the truth and respond to everything. That is why there are always contradictory answers to all premature questions.

The principles above are not the result of a personal opinion but a forceful consequence of the conditions in which the Spirits manifest. It is clear that if a Spirit says something on one side while millions of others say the opposite elsewhere the presumption of truth cannot be on the side of only one or only a few. The pretension of being the only one to be right from the part of the Spirits is as much illogical as it is to a person. When the truly wise Spirits don't feel sufficiently clarified about an issue they never resolve it in absolute terms; the openly indicate to be responding according to their personal opinion and even advise to wait for the confirmation.

However beautiful, fair and great an idea may be, it is impossible to have the opinion of everybody behind it since the beginning. The resulting conflicts are an inevitable consequence of the general movement that takes place; these are even necessary to highlight the truth and it is useful that they take place in the beginning so that the false ideas be promptly discarded. The Spiritists that have some concern must rest assured. All of the isolated pretenses will fall by the force of things before the great and powerful criteria of the universal control.

It is not the opinion of a person that they will follow, but the unanimous voice of the Spirits. It is not a man and more importantly not us more than others that will find the Spiritist orthodoxy; it is not a Spirit that will impose upon anybody either; it is the universality of the Spirits, communicating all over Earth and commanded by God. That is the essential character of the Spiritist Doctrine, its strength and authority. God wanted Its law to be founded on an unbreakable basis and that is why it was not laid upon the fragile mind of a single person.

It is before such a powerful Areopagus[12] that does not know little groups or envious rivalries or sects or nations that every opposition will break, as all the ambitions and pretensions to individual supremacy; that we would ourselves be shattered if we wanted to replace the sovereign designs by our own ideas. It is the only one that will solve all the disputes; that will break

12 [Trans. note] The Areopagus is a prominent rock outcropping located northwest of the Acropolis in Athens, Greece. It literally meant the rock of Ares in the city and was a center of temples, cultural facilities, and a high court.

the dissidences and will give or not give reason to the one that deserves it. Before such power agreement between all voices of heavens what can the opinion of a single person or Spirit do? Less than the drop of water in the whole ocean. Less than the voice of a child muffled by the storm.

The universal opinion that is the supreme judge, the one that has the last word. It is formed by all individual opinions; if one is true it will only have its relative weight on the scale; if it is false it will not be able to succeed against all others. Individuals fade away in that immense assembly and that is a new drawback to human pride.

Such a harmonious horizon is already forming. This century shall not be over before its full resplendence shines out reassuring uncertainties for until then powerful voices would have been assigned the mission of being heard to rank humanity under the same flag as long as the field is sufficiently prepared. While we wait, the one that floats between two opposing systems can observe the direction of the general opinion. That is the correct indication given by the majority of the Spirits about the several points in their communications. It is not a less certain signal about which system will succeed.

May 1864
American Spiritist School

Some people have asked why the Spiritist Doctrine is not the same in the old as well as in the new continent and what is the difference. It is what we are going to try to explain.

As everyone knows the manifestations took place everywhere both in Europe as well as in America and in these days that people are more aware of that they remember a large number of events that had gone unnoticed and that are abundantly registered in authentic texts. Those facts, nonetheless, were isolated. They have recently produced in the United States in a much ample scale to call people's attention on both sides of the Atlantic. The extreme freedom that exists in that country favored the flourishment of the new ideas and that is why the Spirits chose that country as the first theater for their teachings.

Well, it is common that an idea be born in one country and develops in another as we see in sciences and technology. The American intelligence gave proof of that and must not envy Europe in any way. However, if that country sticks out in all matters of commerce and mechanical arts, they must not deny Europe its prominence in moral and philosophical sciences. Due to that difference in the normal features of the peoples experimental Spiritism was in its habitat in America while the theoretical and philosophical part found in Europe a more adequate environment for its development. That is how it was born there and soon conquered it in the first place. The facts there initially attracted curiosity but as soon as curiosity was satisfied people got tired of the material experiments without positive results. The same did not happen from the time when the moral consequences of those events for the future of humanity unfolded. It was the time when Spiritism found its place among philosophical sciences. It advanced at gigantic strides despite the obstacles that were placed on its path because it satisfies the aspirations of the masses and because it was promptly understood that it had come to fill up the immense void of beliefs and resolve what up until then seemed insoluble.

Thus, America was the crib of Spiritism but it was in Europe that it was raised and made its humanities. Should America be jealous for that? No, because there was an advantage in other aspects. Wasn't it in Europe that the steam engine was born and wasn't in America that it found better conditions? Each one has their role according to their skills and each people theirs according to their own particular ingenuity.

What particularly distinguishes the American Spiritist School from the European one is the predominance of phenomena in the former more specially related to that and the latter that is more relate to the philosophical part. The Spiritist philosophy from Europe spread straight away because it offered a consolidated theory since the beginning; because it showed the objective and incontestably broadened the horizon of the ideas and that is the one that prevails today in the whole world. Up until now in the USA they have not moved away from the primitive ideas. Does it mean that they will remain alone in the back end of the general movement? That would be an offense to the intelligence of that people. As a matter of fact, the Spirits are there to push them in the common avenue giving them the teachings that they give somewhere else. They will gradually overcome the resistances that may arise from a national pride. If the Americans repel the European theory because it came from Europe they will accept it when it shows up in their environment by the voice of the Spirits themselves. They will give in not to the opinion of a few people but to the universal control of the Spirits, this powerful criterial as demonstrated in our article about the authority of the Spiritist Doctrine. It is just a matter of time particularly when personal issues have disappeared.

From all principles of Spiritism, the one that found the most opposition in America, and by America here we only mean the USA, is that of reincarnation. It can even be said that this is the only fundamental divergence because the others are more related to the format than the meaning and that because this has not been taught yet by the Spirits there and we have already explained why. The Spirits proceed with wisdom and caution everywhere. They avoid abruptly shocking pre-established ideas to have their own accepted. The dogma of reincarnation in the USA would crash against prejudices of color that are so much entrenched in that country. The essential was to have the fundamental principle of the communication between the visible and invisible world accepted. Issues of detail would come at the right time. There is no doubt that such an obstacle will end up disappearing and that one of the results of the current Civil War will be a gradual weakening of prejudices that are an anomaly in such a liberal nation.

If the idea of reincarnation is not widely accepted in the USA, it is by some if not as an absolute principle at least with certain restrictions, and that it is already something. As for the Spirits they already start to teach that principle in certain places undoubtedly seeing that the moment is adequate and in other places more open. Once the issue is raised it will follow its own course. In fact, we have in our hands old communications received in that country in which without being formally expressed the plurality of the existences is the obvious consequence of the principles that were taught. The idea can be seen under development there. Therefore, there is no doubt that what is called American school today will soon merge with the great unity that is established everywhere.

As a proof of the statements above we will cite the article below published in the *Union*, a San Francisco journal with a summary of the letter that followed it.

"Dear Mr. Allan Kardec,

Although I did not have the honor of getting to know you, as a medium, I take the liberty of sending you the attached news that those gentlemen from the newspaper summarized a bit. Despite that, however, lots of people seem to want more. All of your books, therefore, spread out and our bookstores will soon have to place new orders.

Sincerely,

Pauline Boulay

"News about Spiritism

One does not need more than say something out loud that not everyone understands to be treated as deranged, extravagant or mad. One does not need to be a wise person to write something that comes from the soul and from the heart.

A person of strong personality asked a lady medium:

    — *How come you, an intelligent person, believe in invisible Spirits and in the plurality of the existences? To which the lady replied:*

    — *Maybe I believe because I am intelligent; what I feel gives me more inspiration than what I see for what we see sometimes is deceitful but what we feel does not ever deceive us. You are free to not believe. Those that believe in the plurality of the existences are not bad people and are more selfless than the ones that don't believe. The nonbelievers call them mad people but that does not prove that they tell the truth, on the contrary, for doubting God's power is an offense and denying the existence of something that we cannot touch is an insult to the Creator.*

    — *When something extraordinary happen to us we usually attribute that to chance. Here is my question: what is chance? Nothing, responds the voice of truth. Since the void cannot produce something whatever does exist must come from a productive source. It would be very fair to think that what happens independent of our will must be the works of the Providence directed by the Lord of our destines.*

    — *Irrespectively of what you say and irrespectively of what you do, strong minds, you will never destroy this Doctrine that has always existed. The ignorance of primitive souls imagine that it is all over after this life since they cannot fully understand it. That is mistake! We, the more or less advanced mediums, will finally convince you.*

—   *Spiritism is not only a consolation; it also develops intelligence; destroy every egoistic and greedy thought; puts us in contact with the loved ones and prepares progress, an immense progress that with time will destroy abuse, revolutions and wars.*

—   *The soul does need to reincarnate to improve. It cannot learn everything to understand the works of the Almighty in a single material life. The body is just a temporary envelope in which God sends the soul to advance and endure the necessary trials to its own development and to the realization of the great work of the Creator that we all are called to serve when we are done with our trials and acquired the perfections. All of our contemporary celebrities are another group of souls that progressed through renovated incarnations. Many among them are writing mediums, geniuses that in every new existence bring progress to science and arts.*

—   *The list of geniuses grows every year. These are so many other guides that God brings to our environment to enlighten and educate us, in a word, to teach us what we ignore and that is absolutely necessary to know. They show us the social ulcer; try to destroy our prejudices; bring to the light and before our eyes all the wickedness produced by selfishness and ignorance. These geniuses are animated by superior Spirits. They have done more for progress and civilization than all of your rifles and canyons and bring to our faces more tears of kindness and recognition than everything you have done with your weapons.*

—   *Think seriously about Spiritism, intelligent people, and you will find great teachings there. There is no charlatanism in that great divine law. Everything there is beautiful, great and sublime. It only tends to lead us to perfection and to the true moral happiness.*

— *The book written by mediums and dictated by superior Spirits is a book of high philosophy and in as much subtle as profound teaching. It handles everything. It is true that not everyone is ready for that belief and that to understand it the soul must have reincarnated several times.*

— *When everybody understands Spiritism better our great poets will be better appreciated and read with more attention and respect. Every writer will be understood and admired by all peoples and without envy because causes and effects will be known.*

— *The study of science is the noblest occupation and Spiritism is its divinity. We associate ourselves to the genius through Spiritism and as said by one of our scientists after the genius comes the one that understands the genius.*

— *Education does to the Spirit what a skillful jeweler does to the diamond, polishing it, bringing out the enchanting and seducing charm, enhancing its value.*

— *The soul has not shape as to speak. It is like a spark that changes according to its intensity and according to the degree of acquired perfection. The more it progresses, the more it shines.*

— *When all of you are mediums you will be able to deal with the Spirits as we already do and they will tell you that they are happier than us. They see us, hear us and attend our gatherings, talk to us during the sleep, transport from place to place and are everywhere according to God's wishes.*

Pauline Boulay"

NOTE: The principle of reincarnation is equally found in a manuscript that was sent to us from Montreal, Canada, that we will talk about in the near future.

Reference

Bibliography

BOOKS BY ALLAN KARDEC

KARDEC, Allan. *Genesis, Miracles and Predictions.* Trans. H. M. Monteiro. New York: USSF, 2019.

——————. *The Gospel according to Spiritism.* Trans. H. M. Monteiro. New York: USSF, 2020.

——————. *Heaven and Hell.* Trans. Trans. H. M. Monteiro. New York: USSF, to be published by 2021.

——————. *The Mediums' Book.* Trans. H. M. Monteiro. New York: USSF, 2020.

——————. *The Spirits' Book.* Trans. N. Alves, J. Korngold, H. M. Monteiro. 3rd ed. New York: USSC/USSF, 2020.

——————. *Spiritist Journey in 1862.* Trans H. M. Monteiro. New York: USSF, 2019.

——————. *The Spiritist Review –1858.* Trans L. A. V. Cheim, J. Korngold. New York: USSC/USSF, 2015.

——————. *The Spiritist Review –1859.* Trans L. A. V. Cheim, J. Korngold, J. C. Madden. New York: USSC/USSF, 2015.

——————. *The Spiritist Review –1860.* Trans L. A. V. Cheim, J. Korngold, J. C. Madden. New York: USSC/USSF, 2016.

——————. *The Spiritist Review –1861.* Trans L. A. V. Cheim, J. Korngold. 2nd ed. New York: USSF, 2018.

——————. *The Spiritist Review –1862.* Trans L. A. V. Cheim, J. Korngold, J. C. Madden. 2nd ed. New York: USSF, 2019.

——————. *The Spiritist Review –1863.* Trans L. A. V. Cheim, J. Korngold, J. C. Madden. New York: USSF, 2020.

Note: In 2020 and following years, the five remaining volumes of The Spiritist Review, comprising all issues from years 1864–1868 are scheduled to be published in brand-new English translations by the USSF in New York.

UNITED STATES
SPIRITIST FEDERATION
New York – USA

Book portal: https://is.gd/ussf1

www.ingramcontent.com/pod-product-compliance
Lightning Source LLC
LaVergne TN
LVHW051630080426
835511LV00016B/2278